Hats

Hats

GUILD OF MASTER CRAFTSMAN PUBLICATIONS

First published 2011 by
Guild of Master Craftsman Publications Ltd
Castle Place, 166 High Street,
Lewes, East Sussex, BN7 1XU

Copyright in the Work © GMC Publications Ltd, 2011

ISBN 978-1-86108-866-6

A catalogue record for this book is available from the
British Library.

Publisher: Jonathan Bailey
Production Manager: Jim Bulley
Managing Editor: Gerrie Purcell
Senior Project Editor: Wendy McAngus
Editor: Judith Durant
Managing Art Editor: Gilda Pacitti
Designer: Ginny Zeal

Set in Gill Sans

Colour origination by GMC Reprographics
Printed and bound in China by C & C Offset

Why we love hats

YOU CAN NEVER HAVE ENOUGH HATS. NOT ONLY ARE they excellent for hiding unruly hair or hair that's long gone astray, or for keeping you toasty warm on a cold winter's day, they are also fabulous head-turners. 'If you want to get ahead and get noticed, then get a hat,' as the saying goes.

A hat is the most noticeable fashion item anyone can wear because it draws the onlooker's attention to the face. So top off your outfit with a colourful creation, and hold your head high so people can admire your crowning glory.

From the stylish trilby and the attention-grabbing cloche hat to the casual beanie and functional peaked cap, there is a hat to go with almost any outfit. And with a boundless range of designs, colours and unique twists available there's a hat out there to suit everyone's tastes. The only problem is there are so many hats, but you can only wear one at a time!

Contents

 25

 26

27

 28

29

30

Midnight blue with bobbles and beads, this beanie is topped with teardrop beading on the crown. It is particularly suitable for wearing during the evening.

Nocturne

Size

One size fits most

Actual measurements

20½in (52cm) circumference, 7in (18cm) height

Materials

Sirdar Wash 'n' Wear Double Crepe DK 55% acrylic, 45% nylon (296yds/270m per 100g ball):

1 ball in 0224 Blue

A box each of 4mm pearls (small) and 5mm pearls (large) in Sunrise

A box of 6 x 9mm oval drop pearls in Sunrise

A set each of 3.25mm (UK10:US3) and 4mm (UK8:US6) double-pointed needles

Darning needle

Beading needle

Invisible thread

Tension

19 sts and 25 rows to 4in (10cm) over st st using 4mm needles. Use larger or smaller needles if necessary to obtain correct tension.

Special abbreviations

MB (make bobble): Knit into the front, back, and front again of next st (3 sts), turn and p3, turn and k3, turn and p2tog, p1 (2 sts), turn and sl 1, k1, psso (1 st).

PB (place bead): Bring yarn forward, slip 1 st p-wise, slide up bead, bring yarn to back, leaving the bead in front of slipped st.

Pattern notes

Before starting, thread 8 small, then 8 large beads onto the yarn (large will be knitted first).

To prevent the dpns from twisting as each division of stitches is cast on, clip the needles together with pegs until ready to join.

Hat

Cast on 106 stitches using thumb method and 3.25mm dpns (splitting the sts evenly across 4 needles). Slip the first stitch on the left needle to the right needle and then lift the first stitch on the right needle over this to prevent a 'step' when working in the round (105 sts). Change to 4mm dpns.

Rounds 1, 3 and 5: *K1, p1; rep from * to last st, k1.

Rounds 2 and 4: *P1, k1; rep from * to last st, p1.

Rounds 6–8: Knit, dec 1 st on last round (104 sts).

Round 9: K6, MB, *k12, MB, repeat from * to last 6 sts, k6 (8 bobbles with 12 sts between each one).

Rounds 10–12: Knit.

Round 13: K6, PB *k12, PB repeat from * to last 6 sts, k6 (8 beads with 12 sts between each one).

Rounds 14–16: Knit.

Round 17: As round 13.

Continue working each round in knit until work measures 4½in (11cm) from beg.

Shape crown

Round 1: K5, *sl2, k1, psso, k10, rep from * to last 8 sts sl2, k1, psso, k5 (88 sts).

Rounds 2–4: Knit.

Round 5: K4, *sl2, k1, psso, k8, rep from * to last 7 sts sl2, k1, psso, k4 (72 sts).

Rounds 6–8: Knit.

Round 9: K3, *sl2, k1, psso, k6, rep from * to last 6 sts sl2, k1, psso, k3 (56 sts).

Rounds 10–12: K to end.

Round 13: K2, *sl2, k1, psso, k4, rep from * to last 5 sts sl2, k1, psso, k3 (40 sts).

Rounds 14–16: Knit.

Round 17: K1, *sl2, k1, psso, k2, rep from * to last 4 sts sl2, k1, psso, k3 (24 sts).

Rounds 18 and 19: Knit.

Round 20: *K2tog; rep from * to end (12 sts).

Break yarn and thread through remaining 12 sts twice. Draw up tightly and fasten off.

Finishing

Fasten a small bead, a teardrop bead and another small bead between each decrease around the crown using the loop method. Double the thread and pass the loop through the needle, pass the needle from WS to RS, leaving the thread loop on the WS, pass through a bead, then pass back to the WS and through the thread loop. Secure the thread and fasten off after each bead.

The crocheted flower and shimmery yarn make this hat reminiscent of a 1920s cloche. It is worked circularly, and the brooch can be positioned wherever you fancy for best effect.

Crocheted sparkler

Size

One size fits most

Actual measurements

19½in (50cm) circumference

Materials

Rowan Shimmer 60% cupro, 40% polyester (191yds/175m per 25g ball):

2 balls in 095 Jet

Rowan Kidsilk Haze 70% super kid mohair, 30% silk (229yds/210m per 25g ball):

1 ball in 599 Wicked

3.5mm (UK9:USE/4) crochet hook

Darning needle

Brooch bar

Tension

18 sts and 12 rounds to 4in (10cm) over htr using 3.5mm hook and both yarns together.

Use larger or smaller hook if necessary to obtain correct tension.

Method

The hat is crocheted with both yarns worked together in continuous rounds of half treble stitches. The bottom edge is folded to the inside and stitched in place. The corsage is made by working a chain and slip stitching into each chain stitch. Repeat the process to create the floral fronds, which are coiled up and stitched. By adding a brooch bar, the corsage can be pinned wherever the wearer pleases.

Hat

Using both yarns together, work 4 ch and join with ss to form a ring.

Round 1: Work 6 htr into ring.

Round 2: Work 2 htr into each st (12 sts).

Round 3: (2 htr into next st, 1 htr into next st) 6 times (18 sts).

Round 4: (2 htr into next st, 1 htr into next st) 9 times (27 sts).

Round 5: (2 htr into next st, 1 htr into next 2 sts) 9 times (36 sts).

Round 6: (2 htr into next st, 1 htr into next 3 sts) 9 times (45 sts).

Round 7: (2 htr into next st, 1 htr into next 4 sts) 9 times (54 sts).

Round 8: (2 htr into next st, 1 htr into next 5 sts) 9 times (63 sts).

Round 9: (2 htr into next st, I htr into next 6 sts) 9 times (72 sts).

Round 10: (2 htr into next st, I htr into next 7 sts) 9 times (81 sts).

Round 11: (2 htr into next st, I htr into next 8 sts) 9 times (90 sts).

Round 12: (2 htr into next st, I htr into next 9 sts) 9 times (99 sts).

Round 13: I htr into each st.

Rounds 14–23: Continue without shaping, working I htr into each st.

Round 24: (Htr2tog, I htr in next 9 sts) 9 times (90 sts).

Round 25: (Htr2tog, I htr in next 8 sts) 9 times (81 sts).

Round 26: (Htr2tog, I htr in next 7 sts) 9 times (72 sts).

Round 27: (Htr2tog, I htr in next 6 sts) 9 times (63 sts).

Round 28: Work I htr into each st. Continue without shaping for another 5 rounds. Ss to next st and fasten off.

Finishing

Turn under 3 rounds and ss the edge to the inside of the hat.

Corsage

With both yarns together and 3.5mm hook, make 21 ch.

Ss into 2nd ch from hook, ss to end, turn.

Skip I ch, ss into back loop of next 2 sts.

*Work 17 ch, ss into 2nd ch from hook, ss to end, turn.

Skip I st, ss into back loop of next 2 sts. Rep from * until there are 40 'petals'. Fasten off leaving a long length of yarn. Thread the end onto a needle and, coiling the petals as you go, stitch them in place to form the flower. Sew a brooch bar to the base and pin to the hat.

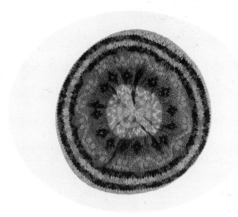

Worked in the round, this traditional Fair Isle pattern uses eight closely related colours, but only two per round. Wear the tam to one side or to the back of the head as you prefer.

Fair Isle tam

Size
One size fits most
Actual measurements
Approximately 22in (56cm) circumference

Materials
Cascade 220, 100% Peruvian Highland wool (220yds/200m per 100g skein):
1 skein in 9076 Mint (A)
1 skein in 9427 Duck Egg Blue (B)

1 skein in 7812 Lagoon (C)
1 skein in 7813 Jade (D)
1 skein in 5018 Summerdaze (E)
1 skein in 9455 Turquoise Heather (F)
1 skein in 2433 Pacific (G)
1 skein in 4009 Teal (H)
4.5mm (UK7:US7) 16in (40cm) circular needle
A set of 4.5mm (UK7:US7) double-pointed needles
Stitch markers (optional)
Darning needle

Fair Isle chart

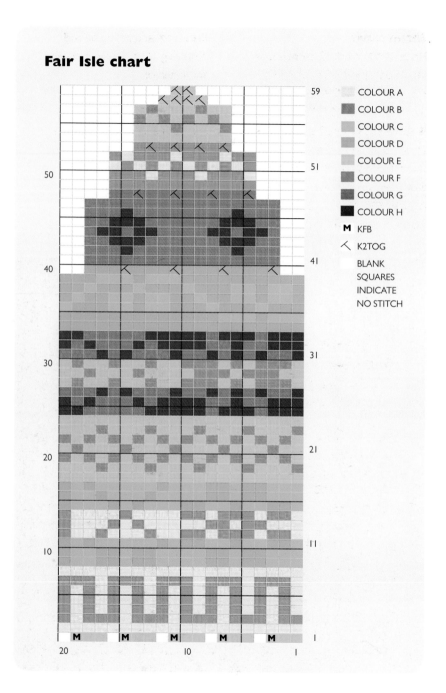

▨	COLOUR A
▨	COLOUR B
▨	COLOUR C
▨	COLOUR D
▨	COLOUR E
▨	COLOUR F
▨	COLOUR G
■	COLOUR H
M	KFB
⋏	K2TOG
☐	BLANK SQUARES INDICATE NO STITCH

Tension

20 sts and 28 rows to 4in (10cm) over st st using 4.5mm needles and lightly blocked.

Special abbreviations

kfb: Increase 1 stitch by knitting into the front and back of the next stitch.

Pattern note

The pattern can be knitted with either a circular needle or a set of double-pointed needles. If using a circular needle, change to double-pointed for the last few decrease rows.

Tam

Cast on 120 stitches and join to work in the round. Work in corrugated rib as follows:

Round 1: *K2 in E, p2 in D, rep from * to end of round.

Rep this round four more times.

Commence chart pattern

Starting with row 1 on the chart and reading from right to left on every round, cont in st st as follows:

Round 1: Using E *k2, kfb, rep from * to end of round (160 sts).

Rounds 2–39: Continue working from chart, changing colours as indicated. You may find it helpful to place stitch markers between each chart repeat (every 20 sts).

Shape crown

Round 40: Work 32 decreases as shown on chart (128 sts).

Round 48: Work 32 decreases as shown on chart (96 sts).

Round 53: Work 32 decreases as shown on chart (64 sts).

Round 58: Work 32 decreases as shown on chart (32 sts).

Round 59: Work 16 decreases as shown on chart (16 sts).

Break yarn and thread through remaining 16 sts. Draw up tightly and fasten off.

Finishing

Weave in ends and block over a dinner plate.

A simple stocking-stitched hat becomes an attention-getter with the addition of a cheery cherry and leaf motif. The cherries become jauntily 3-D when filled with toy stuffing.

Cherry bright

Size

One size fits most

Actual measurements

19¾in (50cm) circumference, 7⅞in (20cm) height

Materials

Rowan Kidsilk Haze 70% super kid mohair, 30% silk (229yds/210m per 25g ball):
1 ball in 597 Jelly (A)
Rowan Siena 4 Ply 100% mercerized cotton (153yds/140m per 50g ball):
Oddments in 671 Alpine (B) and 666 Chilli (C)
A pair each of 3.25mm (UK10:US3), 4mm (UK8:US6) and 2.25mm (UK13:US1) needles
Darning needle
Small amount of soft toy stuffing

Tension

22 sts and 30 rows to 4in (10cm) over st st using 4mm needles and A.

Use larger or smaller needles if necessary to obtain correct tension.

Method

This hat begins with a garter stitch and eyelet border, and then the main piece is worked in stocking stitch. The cherries are knitted then stuffed, and they hang freely from the leaves. Different textured yarns are used for the hat and the decoration.

Hat

Using 3.25mm needles and A, cast on 112 sts.

Work 1¼in (3cm) in garter st, ending on WS row.

Change to 4mm needles.

Row 1 (RS): Knit.

Row 2: Purl.

Row 3: K1, (yf, k2tog) 55 times, k1.

Row 4: Purl.

Continue in stocking st for 34 rows starting with a knit row.

Shape crown

Row 1 (RS): (k6, k2tog) 14 times (98 sts).

Work 3 rows stocking st.

Row 5 (RS): (k5, k2tog) 14 times (84 sts).

Work 3 rows stocking st.

Row 9 (RS): (k4, k2tog) 14 times (70 sts).

Work 3 rows stocking st.

Row 13 (RS): (k3, k2tog) 14 times (56 sts).

Row 14: Purl.

Row 15 (RS): (k2tog) 28 times (28 sts).

Row 16: Purl.

Break yarn and thread through remaining 28 sts. Draw up tightly and fasten off.

Leaf and stalk
(make 2)

Using 2.25mm needles and B, cast on 2 sts leaving a long length of the yarn to sew on the cherry later. Pass first st over second st, 1 st remains on the needle.

*Cast on 1 st, pass previous st over new st. Rep from * 3 more times. This forms the stalk.

To make the leaf cast on 2 sts (3 sts).

Row 1 (WS): Purl

Row 2: K1, yf, k1, yf, k1 (5 sts).

Row 3 and every WS row: Purl.

Row 4: K2, yf, k1, yf, k2 (7 sts).

Row 6: K3, yf, k1, yf, k3 (9 sts).

Row 8: K4, yf, k1, yf, k4 (11 sts).

Row 10: K2tog tbl, k to last 2 sts, k2tog (9 sts).

Continue dec in this way at each end of every RS row until 3 sts remain, ending with a purl row.

Next row: Sl 1, k2 tog, psso.

Fasten off leaving a long length of yarn with which to stitch the leaf to the hat.

Cherries
(make 2)

Using 2.25mm needles and C, cast on 3 sts.

Row 1 (RS): Knit into front and back of each st (6 sts).

Row 2: Purl.

Rows 3–6: Rep rows 1 and 2 twice (24 sts).

Row 7 (RS): Knit.

Row 8: Purl.

Row 9: K2tog to end (12 sts).

Row 10: Purl.

Row 11: K2tog to end (6 sts).

Row 12: Purl.

Break yarn and thread through remaining 6 sts. Draw up tightly and stitch the side seam, stuffing the cherry as you sew before fastening off. Sew in yarn ends.

Making up

Neatly stitch together the seam of the hat. Sew the leaves in place on the hat joining the tops of the stems with a couple of stitches at the same time. Sew the cherries on to each stem using the long length of yarn you left at the beginning.

Cables to the right, cables to the left, cables to the centre – there are patterns aplenty in this cozy cap. The band is knitted flat and seamed, and the crown is picked up and worked in the round.

Purple cables

Size
One size fits most

Actual measurements
22½in (57cm) circumference

Materials
King Cole Big Value Chunky 100% acrylic (167yds/152m per 100g ball):
2 balls in 556 Heather
A pair of 3.5mm (US4) needles
3.5mm (US4) 24in (60cm) circular needle
A set of 3.5mm (US4) double-pointed needles
Darning needle
Stitch markers

Purple cable chart

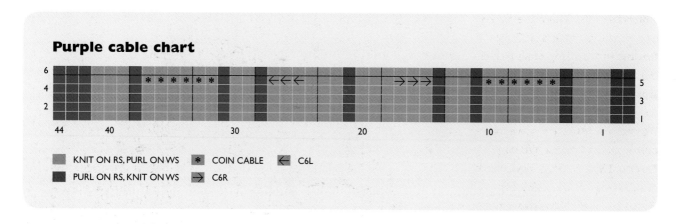

KNIT ON RS, PURL ON WS
PURL ON RS, KNIT ON WS
* COIN CABLE
← C6L
→ C6R

Tension

38 sts and 20 rows to (4in) 10cm over cable pattern.

Use larger or smaller needles if necessary to obtain correct tension.

Special abbreviations

Coin cable: (over 6 sts) Sl 5 sts to cable needle (cn) and hold at back of work, k1, sl last 4 sts from cn back onto left-hand needle, k4, k1 from cn.

C6B: (over 6 sts) Sl 3 sts to cn and hold at back of work, k3, k3 from cn.

C6F: (over 6 sts) Sl 3 sts to cn and hold at front of work, k3, k3 from cn.

Pattern note

Change to double-pointed needles for the last few decreases on the crown, or if preferred use for the whole crown.

Cable band

(this will be turned sideways when completed)

Cast on 44 sts using straight needles. Commence with cable pattern following either the chart or the written instructions below.

Row 1 (RS): P2, k3, p1, k6, p1, k2, p1, k6, p1, k6, p1, k2, p1, k6, p1, k3, p1.

Row 2: K1, p3, k1, p6, k1, p2, k1, p6, k1, p6, k1, p2, k1, p6, k1, p3, k2.

Rows 3 & 4: Repeat rows 1 and 2.

Row 5: P2, k3, p1, coin cable, p1, k2, p1, C6B p1, C6F, p1, k2, p1, coin cable, p1, k3, p1.

Row 6: Repeat row 2.

These 6 rows set the cable pattern. Repeat rows 1–6 (22 times), then rep rows 1–3 once more. Work measures approx. 23in (58.5cm).

Cast off loosely in pattern.

Making up

With RS facing turn under the two purl sts down the right-hand side to form a hem and sl st in place (this forms the base of the hat). Place RS together and join the cast-on and cast-off edges of cable band to form a loop.

Crown

With RS of work facing and using circular needle, pick up and knit 140 sts evenly around the top edge of cable band.

Round 1: *K12, k2tog, mark with stitch marker; rep from * to end (130 sts).

Round 2 and every foll alt round through round 16: Knit.

Round 3: *K11, k2tog, move marker over; rep from * to end (120 sts).

Round 5: *K10, k2tog, move marker over; rep from * to end (110 sts).

Round 7: *K9, k2tog, move marker over; rep from * to end (100 sts).
Round 9: *K8, k2tog, move marker over; rep from * to end (90 sts).
Round 11: *K7, k2tog, move marker over; rep from * to end (80 sts).
Round 13: *K6, k2tog, move marker over; rep from * to end (70 sts).
Round 15: *K5, k2tog, move marker over; rep from * to end (60 sts).
Round 17: *K4, k2tog, move marker over; rep from * to end (50 sts).
Round 18: *K3, k2tog, move marker over; rep from * to end (40 sts).
Round 19: *K2, k2tog, move marker over; rep from * to end (30 sts).
Round 20: *K1, k2tog, move marker over; rep from * to end (20 sts).
Round 21: *K2tog, remove marker; rep from * to end (10 sts).
Break off the yarn leaving a long end, thread through the remaining 10 stitches and fasten off on the wrong side.

Flexibility is the name of the game with this beanie. Wear it stretched down and pulled over your ears, or scrunched up and perched on top of your head – whatever suits your mood or the weather.

Beehive beanie

Size
One size fits most

Actual measurements
18⅞in (48cm) circumference, 6¾in (17cm) height without stretching

Materials
Rowan Pure Wool DK, 100% wool (137yds/125m per 50g ball):
2 balls in 007 Cypress
A pair each of 3.25mm (UK10:US3) and 4mm (UK8:US6) needles
Darning needle

Tension

22 sts and 30 rows to 4in (10cm) over st st using 4mm needles. Use larger or smaller needles if necessary to obtain correct tension.

Method

The beanie is worked in rows of regular and reverse stocking stitch to create the beehive shape. Stitches are decreased at the crown, and the cap is seamed up the back. The knitted piece, when stretched, is longer than the finished length, so it requires a few more rows and a little more yarn than a simple beanie.

Hat

Using 3.25mm needles, cast on 114 sts. Work 8 rows in garter st. Change to 4mm needles.

Row 1 (WS): Knit.
Row 2: Purl.
Rep last 2 rows twice.
Row 7: Knit.
Row 8: Knit.
Row 9: Purl.
Rows 10–13: Rep rows 8 and 9 twice.
Rows 14–34: Rep rows 7–13 three times.

Shape crown

Row 35: (K17, k2tog) 6 times (108 sts).
Row 36: Knit.
Row 37: Purl.
Rows 38–41: Rep rows 36 and 37 twice.
Row 42: (K10, k2tog) 9 times (99 sts).
Row 43: Knit.
Row 44: Purl.
Rows 45–48: Rep rows 43 and 44 twice.
Row 49: (K9, k2tog) 9 times (90 sts).
Row 50: Knit.
Row 51: Purl.
Rows 52–55: Rep rows 50 and 51 twice.
Row 56: (K4, k2tog) 15 times (75 sts).
Row 57: Knit.
Row 58: Purl.
Rows 59–62: Rep rows 57 and 58 twice.
Row 63: (K3, k2tog) 15 times (60 sts).
Row 64: Knit.
Row 65: Purl.
Rows 66–69: Rep rows 64 and 65 twice.
Row 70: (K2, k2tog) 15 times (45 sts).
Row 71: Knit.
Row 72: Purl.

Rows 73–76: Repeat rows 71 and 72 twice.
Row 77: (K1, k2tog) 15 times (30 sts).
Row 78: Knit.
Row 79: Purl.
Rows 80–83: Rep rows 78 and 79 twice.
Row 84: (K2tog) 15 times (15 sts).
Row 85: Knit.
Row 86: Purl.
Rows 87–90: Repeat rows 85 and 86 twice.
Break off yarn and thread through remaining 15 sts. Draw up tightly and fasten off.

Making up

Join the back seam carefully matching the pattern.

It's always springtime when you're wearing this crocheted hat covered with a mass of pretty blossom. Unlike the real thing, these crocheted flowers will always be in bloom.

Cherry blossom

Size

One size fits most

Actual measurements

19½in (50cm) circumference, 7in (18cm) height

Materials

Sublime Organic Merino DK 100% organic merino wool
(113yds/105m per 50g ball):
1 ball in 0113 Twine (A)
1 ball in 0189 Floss (B)
Twilleys Goldfingering 80% viscose, 20% metallized polyester
(110yds/100m per 25g ball):
1 ball in 04 Light Gold (C)
4mm (UK8:USG/6), 3.5mm (UK9:USE/4), and 2.5mm
(UK12:USC/2) crochet hooks
Darning needle

Tension

19 sts and 10 rounds to 4in (10cm) over pattern using 4mm hook.
Use larger or smaller hook if necessary to obtain correct tension.

Method

The main part of the hat is worked in rounds of half treble and chain stitches and in continuous rounds after the shaping is complete. It is decorated with more than 60 crocheted blossoms, which are stitched to the basic shape.

Hat

Using 4mm hook and A, make 5 ch. Join with ss to form a loop.

Round 1: 3 ch to count as first htr and 1 ch sp, (work 1 htr into loop, 1 ch) 7 times. Join with ss to 2nd of first 3 ch (8 sps).

Round 2: 3 ch to count as first htr and 1 ch sp. Work 1 htr into first ch sp, 1 ch, *(1 htr, 1 ch, 1 htr) into next ch sp, 1 ch. Rep from * to end. Join with a ss to 2nd of first 3 ch (16 sps).

Round 3: 3 ch, work 1 htr into first ch sp, 1 ch, work 1 htr into next 1 ch sp, 1 ch, *(1 htr, 1 ch, 1 htr) into next 1 ch sp, 1 ch, 1 htr into next 1 ch sp, 1 ch. Rep from * to end. Join with ss to 2nd of first 3 ch (24 sps).

Round 4: 3 ch, skip first ch sp, (1 htr into next 1 ch sp, 1 ch) to end. Join with ss to 2nd of first 3 ch.

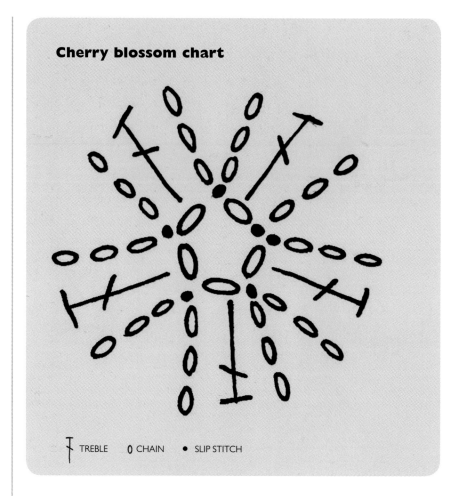

Cherry blossom chart

† TREBLE   O CHAIN   • SLIP STITCH

Round 5: 3 ch, 1 htr into first ch sp, 1 ch, (1 htr into next 1 ch sp, 1 ch) twice, *(1 htr, 1 ch, 1 htr) into next 1 ch sp, 1 ch, (1 htr into next 1 ch sp, 1 ch) twice. Rep from * to end. Join with ss to 2nd of first 3 ch (32 sps).

Round 6: As round 4.

Round 7: 3 ch, work 1 htr into first ch sp, 1 ch, (1 htr into next 1 ch sp, 1 ch) 3 times, *(1 htr, 1 ch, 1 htr) into next 1 ch sp, 1 ch, (1 htr into next 1 ch sp, 1 ch) 3 times. Rep from * to end. Join with ss to 2nd of first 3 ch (40 sps).

Round 8: As round 4.

Round 9: 3 ch, 1 htr into first ch sp, 1 ch, (1 htr into next 1 ch sp, 1 ch) 4 times, *(1 htr, 1 ch, 1 htr) into next

Making up

Stitch the flowers to the hat positioning 3 around the top, 8 around the first 3, 12 on the next row, 13 on each of the next 2 rows and 14 around the lower edge.

Blossom centres

Using 2.5mm hook and C, make 3 ch. Work 3 tr tog into first ch by leaving the last loop of each st on the hook (4 loops on hook), yarn over hook, draw through all 4 loops, ss to first ch. Fasten off leaving a long length of yarn and stitch to the middle of the flower. Repeat until all the blossoms have gold centres.

1 ch sp, 1 ch, (1 htr into next 1 ch sp, 1 ch) 4 times. Rep from * to end. Join with ss to 2nd of first 3 ch (48 sps).
Round 10: 3 ch, skip first ch sp, *(1 htr into next 1 ch sp, 1 ch). Rep from * working in continuous rounds until the hat measures 7in (18cm) and the yarn has run out. Fasten off and sew in the ends.

Blossoms
(make approximately 63 using all the yarn)

Using 3.5mm hook and B, leave a long length of yarn at beginning and make 5 ch. Join with ss to form a loop.
Next round: (3 ch, 1 tr into the loop, 3 ch, ss into the loop) 5 times. Fasten off.

This soft, chunky hat can be worn pulled down with a convex crown or high on the head with the crown indented. The detachable flower brooch may be pinned to either style, wherever you like.

Aurora

Size

One size fits most. For a smaller size add shirring elastic to the inside.

Actual measurements

21in (53cm) circumference, 7in (18cm) height

Materials

Wendy Serenity Super Chunky, 10% wool, 20% alpaca, 70% acrylic (87½yds/80m per 100g ball):

1 ball in 1702 Pink

6mm (UK4:US10) circular needle 16in (40cm) long

A set of 6mm (UK4:US10) double-pointed needles

A box of Craft Factory 5mm pearls in Pale Orange

14in (35cm) of cream antique lace or embellishment of choice

¾in (2cm) brooch pin or tiny gold safety pin

Stitch markers

Darning, beading and sewing needles

Clear sewing thread

Tension

11.5 sts and 16 rows to 4in (10cm) over st st.

Use larger or smaller needles to obtain correct tension.

Special abbreviations

m1r (make one right-leaning stitch): Find the horizontal connecting yarn between the needles. Using the left needle, pick up the connecting yarn *from the back to the front* and leave this 'raised bar' on the left needle. Work the raised bar by knitting (RS row) or purling (WS row) as appropriate.

m1l (make one left-leaning stitch): Find the horizontal connecting yarn between the needles. Using the left needle, pick up the connecting yarn *from the front to the back* and leave this 'raised bar' on the left needle. Then either knit the raised bar through the back of the loop (RS row) or purl the raised bar (WS row).

Pattern note

Double-pointed needles can be used throughout if preferred.

Hat

Using circular needle cast on 61 stitches with the thumb method. Slip the first stitch on the left needle onto the right needle and then lift the first stitch on the right needle over and off the needle to prevent a 'step' when working in the round (60 sts).

Round 1: Purl.
Round 2: Knit.
Round 3: Purl.
Round 4: *K1, sl, k1, k3, rep from * to end.
Round 5: *P1, k1, p1, k3, rep from * to end.

Rep rounds 4 and 5 until the work measures 4in (10cm) or it is possible to count 7 slipped chains from the bottom to the top. Work round 4 once more.

Next round: Purl.
Next round: Knit.

Shape crown

Each round is decreased by 6 stitches. Change to double-pointed needles when there are too few stitches to work on circular needle.

Round 1: K2tog, *k8, k2tog, rep from * to last 8 sts, k8 (54 sts).
Round 2 and every foll alt row: K to end.
Round 3: K2tog, *k7, k2tog, rep from * to last 7 sts, k7 (48 sts).
Round 5: K2tog, *k6, k2tog, rep from * to last 6 sts, k6 (42 sts).

Round 7: K2tog, *k5, k2tog, rep from * to last 5 sts, k5 (36 sts).
Round 9: K2tog, *k4, k2tog, rep from * to last 4 sts, k4 (30 sts).
Round 11: K2tog, *k3, k2tog, rep from * to last 3 sts, k3 (24 sts).
Round 13: K2tog, *k2, k2tog, rep from * to last 2 sts, k2 (18 sts).
Round 14: K2tog, rep to end of row (9 sts).

Break yarn and thread through remaining 9 stitches. Draw up tightly and fasten off.

Beaded edging for the hat

Fasten 10 beads around the base of the hat, sandwiching them on the knit row between the two purl rows and at the base of each slip-stitch column with the loop method. Double the thread and pass the loop through the needle, pass the needle from WS to RS, leaving the thread loop on the WS, pass through a bead, then pass back to the WS and through the thread loop. Secure the thread and fasten off after each bead.

Corsage and brooch base
Base

Cast on 3 sts.

Row 1: K1, m1r, k to last st, m1l, k1 (5 sts).

Row 2 and every foll alt row:
P to end.

Row 3: K1, m1r, k to last stitch, m1l, k1 (7 sts).

Row 5: Sl1, k1, psso, k to last 2 sts, k2tog (5 sts).

Row 7: Sl1, k1, psso, k to last 2 sts, k2tog (3 sts).

Cast off k-wise, sew in ends neatly, following the line of the stitches.

Corsage

Using clear thread, over-sew and French seam (wrong sides together seam, then right sides together seam) the two short ends of the piece of lace to form a circle. Sew with running stitch around the inner circle and gather until you have an opening of approx. ½in (1.5cm). Stitch again before securing. Centre the lace on the knitted base and stitch in place around the central hole. Arrange 8 beads in a small circle at the centre of the lace, and add 1 bead in the centre and secure them with the loop method as described above. Stitch the brooch pin in place on the underside of the knitted circle. Pin the corsage onto one of the plain panels.

Named after the main character in George du Maurier's novel-cum-play *Trilby*, this knitted version of the popular hat looks smart on just about anyone. The parts are knitted separately and sewn together.

Trilby

Size
One size fits most

Actual measurements
20in (51cm) circumference

Materials
Rowan Felted Tweed Aran 50% merino wool, 25% alpaca, 25% viscose (95yds/87m per 50g ball):
3 balls in 729 Soot
A pair of 5mm (UK6:US8) needles
Darning needle

Tension

16 sts and 27 rows to 4in (10cm) over moss st.

Use larger or smaller needles if necessary to obtain correct tension.

Method

Each piece is knitted separately then stitched to form the trilby. The brim is made up of two pieces that are sandwiched together to give it shape.

Hat

Sides

(make 2)

Cast on 39 sts.

Work in moss st as follows:

Row 1 (RS): (K1, p1) to last st, k1.

Row 2 (WS): As row 1.

Rep rows 1 and 2 until work measures 5⅛in (13cm) ending with a WS row.

Shaping

Keeping moss st pattern correct, work 2tog at both ends of next and every alt row until there are 33 sts, ending with a WS row, then every row until 23 sts remain. Cast off in moss st.

Top

Cast on 1 st.

Row 1: Inc 1 (2 sts).

Row 2: Inc 1, k1 (3 sts).

Row 3: Inc 1, k1, inc 1 (5 sts).

Row 4: Inc 1, p1, k1, p1, inc 1 (7 sts).

Keeping moss st correct, continue increasing at both ends of every row until there are 13 sts.

Increase 1 st at both ends of every alternate row until there are 17 sts.

Continue in moss st on these 17 sts until work measures 5½in (14cm) from end of shaping.

Work 2tog at both ends of next and following alt row (13 sts).

Work 2tog at both ends of every row until 3 sts remain.

Next row: K2tog, k1 (2 sts).

Next row: K2tog (1 st).

Fasten off.

Brim

Cast on 79 sts.

Row 1 (WS): Knit.

Row 2 (RS): Knit.

Row 3: (Inc 1, k1) to last st, inc 1 (119 sts).

Row 4: K1, (p1, k1) to end.

Rep row 4 until work measures 2⅜in (6cm) from cast-on edge, ending with a WS row.

Break yarn and leave sts on a spare needle.

Rep to make 2nd half of brim but don't break yarn.

Join brim

Hold the 2 needles parallel with WS tog.

Working on RS, ktog a st from each needle which will leave 1 st on the right-hand needle, *ktog the next 2 sts (2 sts on right-hand needle), then pass the 1st of these 2 sts over the 2nd. Rep from * to end.

Making up

Join the straight edges of the sides of the hat. Sew the top in place, matching the shaped edges of the sides. Press the top piece into your hat to give the trilby effect.

Lay the brim out flat and join the two short ends, matching the cast-off edge. Fold the brim at the cast-off sts then sew the two rows of cast-on sts to the lower edge of the hat.

Rectangles join with both horizontal and vertical stripes to fashion this geometric patterned hat in simple and bold red, white and black. A more organically shaped bobble at the top softens the look.

Geometrics

Size

One size fits most

Actual measurements

20½in (52cm) circumference, 8½in (21.5cm) height

Materials

Jamieson's Shetland Spindrift 100% Shetland wool
(115yds/105m per 25g ball):
1 ball in 101 Shetland Black (A)
1 ball in 114 Mooskit/White (B)
1 ball in 525 Crimson (C)
A pair each of 2.75mm (UK12:US2) and 3.25mm (UK10:US3)
needles
Darning needle

Tension

28 sts and 30 rows to 4in (10cm) over pattern using 3.25mm needles. Use larger or smaller needles if necessary to obtain correct tension.

Method

A band of garter stitch is knitted first, then the colours are joined in and the geometric pattern is worked in stocking stitch from the chart. The top of the hat and the crown shaping is finished in one block of colour. The bobble decoration is made simply by casting on and off a number of stitches that are then coiled at the base and stitched in place.

Hat

Using 2.75mm needles and A, cast on 146 sts.

Work 1in (2.5cm) in g st.

Change to 3.25mm needles and follow the 20 st pattern repeat from chart beg on row 1, reading the knit rows (odd numbers) from right to left and the purl rows (even numbers) from left to right. Increase row 3 as follows:

Row 3 (RS): Work 10 sts in patt from chart, m1 using shade B, *pattern 18 sts, m1 using shade B, rep from * to last 28 sts, patt 18 sts, m1, patt to end (154 sts).

Rows 4–16: Work chart rows 4 through 16.

Row 17 (inc): Using shade B, patt 11 from chart, inc 1 by knitting twice into next st, (patt 18, inc 1) to last 10 sts, patt 10 (162 sts).

Rows 18–20: Work chart rows 18 through 20.

Row 21: Work in st st using A until the hat measures 5in (12.5cm) from cast-on edge.

Shape crown

Row 22 (dec): (K7, k2tog) 18 times (144 sts).

Work 3 rows.

Geometrics chart

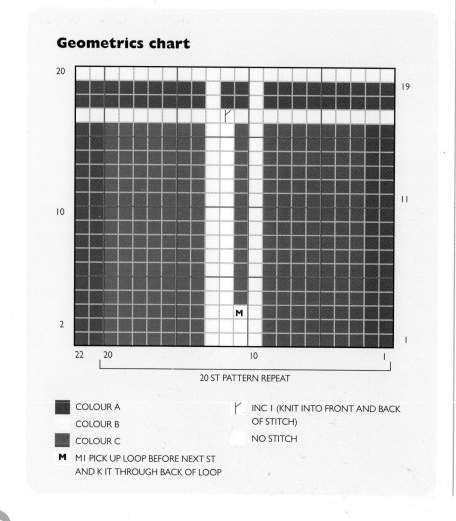

20 ST PATTERN REPEAT

■ COLOUR A
COLOUR B
■ COLOUR C
M M1 PICK UP LOOP BEFORE NEXT ST AND K IT THROUGH BACK OF LOOP

Γ INC 1 (KNIT INTO FRONT AND BACK OF STITCH)

NO STITCH

Row 26 (dec): (K6, k2tog) 18 times (126 sts).
Work 3 rows.
Row 30 (dec): (K5, k2tog) 18 times (108 sts).
Work 3 rows.
Row 34 (dec): (K4, k2tog) 18 times (90 sts).
Work 3 rows.
Row 38 (dec): (K3, k2tog) 18 times (72 sts).
Work 3 rows.
Row 42 (dec): (K2, k2tog) 18 times (54 sts).

Work 1 row.
Row 44 (dec): (k1, k2tog) 18 times (36 sts).
Work 1 row.
Row 46 (dec): (k2tog) 18 times (18 sts).
Work 1 row.
Break yarn and thread through remaining 18 sts. Draw up tightly and fasten off.

Making up

Join the back seam matching the pattern.

Bobble

With 2.75mm needles and C, cast on 15 sts, (cast off 14, cast on another 14 sts so there are 15 on the left-hand needle) 20 times, cast off 15 sts leaving a long length of yarn.
Wind the tail around the base of the bobble and stitch the parts in place as you go, positioning the tassel ends so they point up and out. Sew to the top of the hat.

Crocheted 'fur' covers this cap for a fun and fanciful look
that's perfect for a bad hair day! The 'fur' stays hidden while you're
making the hat, then pops out when you turn it right side out.

Fur fun

Size
One size fits most
Actual measurements
19½in (50cm) circumference

Materials
150g of Aran-weight yarn
4.5mm (UK7:US7) crochet hook
Darning needle

Tension

12 sts and 8 rounds to 4in (10cm) over trebles using 4.5mm hook.
Use larger or smaller hook if necessary to obtain correct tension.

Pattern note

The fur loops will appear on the back of the fabric as you are working.

Method

The hat is worked from the wrong side in rounds of trebles, starting at the crown and increasing stitches to shape. The 'fur' fabric consists of loops made by working chain stitches into the back loops of the previous round of trebles, while the next round of trebles is worked into the front loops of the same stitches. The hat is finished with a brim of trebles.

Hat

Work 4 ch and join with ss to form a ring.

Round 1 (inc): 3 ch to count as first tr, 14 tr into ring, ss to top of 3 ch (15 sts).

Round 2: (10 ch, 1 dc into the back loop only of the next st) to end.

Round 3 (inc): 1 dc into front loop of next st, 3 ch to count as first tr, 1 tr into same st, (2 tr into front loop only of next st), 14 times, ss to top of 3 ch (30 sts).

Round 4: As round 2.

Round 5 (inc): 1 dc into front loop of next st, 3 ch to count as first tr, 1 tr into same st, (1 tr into front loop only of next st, 2 tr into front loop of next st) 14 times, 1 tr into front loop of next st, ss to top of 3 ch (45 sts).

Round 6: As round 2.

Round 7 (inc): 1 dc into front loop of next st, 3 ch to count as first tr, 1 tr into same st, (1 tr into front loop only of next 2 sts, 2 tr into front loop of next st) 14 times, 1 tr into front loop of next 2 sts, ss to top of 3 ch (60 sts).

Round 8: As round 2.

Round 9 (inc): 1 dc into front loop of next st, 3 ch to count as first tr, 1 tr into same st, (1 tr into front loop only of next 9 sts, 2 tr into front loop of next st) 5 times, 1 tr into front loop of next 9 sts, ss to top of 3 ch (66 sts).

Round 10: As round 2.

Round 11: 1 dc into front loop of next st, 3 ch to count as first tr, (1 tr into front loop only of next st) to end, ss to top of 3 ch.

Rounds 12–19: Rep last 2 rounds 4 more times.

Round 20: As round 2.

Round 21 (dec): 1 dc into front loop of next st, 3 ch to count as first tr, 1 tr into front loop of next 8 sts, (work 2trtog into front loops of sts, 1 tr into front loop of next 9 sts) 5 times, work 2trtog into front loops of sts, ss to top of 3 ch (60 sts).

Round 22: 3 ch to count as first tr, 1 tr into both loops of each st to end, ss to top of 3 ch.

Rounds 23–24: Rep last round.

Finishing

Sew in ends.

This intricate-looking hat is easy to knit in stocking and garter stitch – simply slipping certain stitches forms the honeycomb pattern. A small pompom on top accents the look perfectly.

Perky pompom

Size

One size fits most

Actual measurements

18½in (47cm) circumference, 7½in (19cm) height excluding pompom

Materials

Jamieson & Smith Shetland Aran 100% wool (98yds/90m per 50g ball):

1 ball in BSS80 (A)

1 ball in BSS10 (B)

A pair each of 3.75mm (UK9:US5) and 4.5mm (UK7:US7) needles

Darning needle

Thin card to make pompom

Tension

20 sts and 34 rows to 4in (10cm) over pattern using 4.5mm needles. Use larger or smaller needles if necessary to obtain correct tension.

Method

The hat begins with a rib around the lower edge and then continues in a repeated pattern of 2 rows in garter stitch, then 6 rows in stocking stitch with every few stitches being slipped to create the honeycomb pattern. After shaping the crown and joining the seam, a small pompom is attached to the top.

Hat

Using 3.75mm needles, cast on 92 sts. Work 1¼in (3cm) in k1, p1 rib. Change to 4.5mm needles and continue in pattern as follows:

Rows 1 and 2: With A, knit.

Row 3: With B, k1, (sl 2 p-wise, k6) to last 3 sts, sl 2 p-wise, k1.

Row 4: With B, p1, (sl 2 p-wise, p6) to last 3 sts, sl 2 p-wise, p1.

Rows 5–8: Rep rows 3–4 (twice).

Rows 9 and 10: Rep rows 1 and 2.

Row 11: With B, k5, (sl 2 p-wise, k6) to last 7 sts, sl 2 p-wise, k5.

Row 12: With B, p5, (sl 2 p-wise, p6) to last 5 sts, p5.

Rows 13–16: rep rows 11 and 12 (twice).

Rep these 16 rows once more, and then rep the first 8 rows again.

Shape crown

Row 1 (dec): With A, k1, (k2tog, k2) to last 3 sts, k2tog, k1 (69 sts).

Row 2: With A, knit.

Row 3: With B, k4, sl 1 p-wise, (k5, sl 1 p-wise) to last 4 sts, k4.

Row 4: With B, p4, sl 1 p-wise, (p5, sl 1 p-wise) to last 4 sts, p4.

Rows 5–8: Rep rows 3 and 4 twice.

Row 9 (dec): With A, k2, (k2tog, k1) to last st, k1 (47 sts).

Row 10: With A, knit.

Row 11: With B, k1, (sl 1 p-wise, k3) to last 2 sts, sl 1 p-wise, k1.

Row 12: With B, p1, (sl 1 p-wise, p3) to last 2 sts, sl 1 p-wise, p1.

Rows 13–16: Rep rows 11 and 12 twice.

Row 17: With A, knit.

Row 18 (dec): With A, k1, (k2tog) to end (24 sts).

Rows 19 and 20: With A, knit.

Row 21 (dec): With A, (k2tog) 12 times (12 sts).

Work 1 row in A. Break off yarn, thread through rem sts, draw up tightly and fasten off.

Making up

Join the back seam carefully matching the pattern. Make a small pompom (see page 150) and attach to the top of the hat.

The nature of the yarn and the trailing leaf pattern gives this hat a delicate appearance. The fabric is very stretchy, so you can tuck your hair up into the hat, no matter how long it is.

Gold leaf

Size
One size fits most
Actual measurements
14in (36cm) circumference without stretching, 7½in (19cm) height

Materials
125g of any 4-ply (fingering weight) metallic yarn
A pair each of 3.25mm (UK10:US3) and 4mm (UK8:US6) needles
Darning needle

Tension

42 sts and 36 rows to 4in (10cm) over pattern (without stretching) using 4mm needles.
Use larger or smaller needles if necessary to obtain correct tension.

Method

The hat begins with a 3 × 3 rib. The leaf pattern is formed by increasing and decreasing stitches in plain and purl, so the number of stitches will fluctuate as you work.

Hat

Using 3.25mm needles, cast on 133 sts.
Next row (RS): P2, (k3, p3) to last 5 sts, k3, p2.
Next row: K2, (p3, k3) to last 5 sts, p3, k2.
These 2 rows form the rib. Work 1¼in (3cm) in rib.
Change to 4mm needles and work in patt as follows:
Row 1 (RS): P3, (k1, p5) to last 4 sts, k1, p3.
Row 2: K3, (p1, k5) to last 4 sts, p1, k3.
Row 3: P3, (yo, k1, yo, p5, k1, p5) to last 10 sts, yo, k1, yo, p5, k1, p3 (155 sts).
Row 4: K3, (p1, k5, p3, k5) to last 12 sts, p1, k5, p3, k3.

Row 5: P3, (k1, yo, k1, yo, k1, p5, k1, p5) to last 12 sts, k1, yo, k1, yo, k1, p5, k1, p3 (177 sts).
Row 6: K3, (p1, k5, p5, k5) to last 14 sts, p1, k5, p5, k3.
Row 7: P3, (k2, yo, k1, yo, k2, p5, k1, p5) to last 14 sts, k2, yo, k1, yo, k2, p5, k1, p3 (199 sts).
Row 8: K3, (p1, k5, p7, k5) to last 16 sts, p1, k5, p7, k3.
Row 9: P3, (k3, yo, k1, yo, k3, p5, k1, p5) to last 16 sts, k3, yo, k1, yo, k3, p5, k1, p3 (221 sts).
Row 10: K3, (p1, k5, p9, k5) to last 18 sts, p1, k5, p9, k3.
Row 11: P3, (k3, sl 2tog k-wise, k1, p2sso, k3, p5, yo, k1, yo, p5) to last 18 sts, k3, sl 2tog k-wise, k1, p2sso, k3, p5, yo, k1, yo, p3.
Row 12: K3, (p3, k5, p7, k5) to last 18 sts, p3, k5, p7, k3.
Row 13: P3, (k2, sl 2tog k-wise, k1, p2sso, k2, p5, k1, yo, k1, yo, k1, p5) to last 18 sts, k2, sl 2tog k-wise, k1, p2sso, k2, p5, k1, yo, k1, yo, k1, p3.
Row 14: K3, (p5, k5) to last 8 sts, p5, k3.
Row 15: P3, (k1, sl 2tog k-wise, k1, p2sso, k1, p5, k2, yo, k1, yo, k2, p5) to last 18 sts, k1, sl 2tog k-wise, k1, p2sso, k1, p5, k2, yo, k1, yo, k2, p3.
Row 16: K3, (p7, K5, p3, k5) to last 18 sts, p7, k5, p3, k3.

Row 17: P3, (sl 2tog k-wise, k1, p2sso, p5, k3, yo, k1, yo, k3, p5) to last 18 sts, sl 2tog k-wise, k1, p2sso, p5, k3, yo, k1, yo, k3, p3.
Row 18: K3, (p9, k5, p1, k5) to last 18 sts, p9, k5, p1, k3.
Row 19: P3, (yo, k1, yo, p5, k3, sl 2tog k-wise, k1, p2sso, k3, p5) to last 18 sts, yo, k1, yo, p5, k3, sl 2tog k-wise, k1, p2sso, k3, p3.
Row 20: K3, (p7, k5, p3, k5) to last 18 sts, p7, k5, p3, k3.
Row 21: P3, (k1, yo, k1, yo, k1, p5, k2, sl 2tog k-wise, k1, p2sso, k2, p5) to last 18 sts, k1, yo, k1, yo, k1, p5, k2, sl 2tog k-wise, k1, p2sso, k2, p3.
Row 22: K3, (p5, k5) to last 8 sts, p5, k3.
Row 23: P3, (k2, yo, k1, yo, k2, p5, k1, sl 2tog k-wise, k1, p2sso, k1, p5) to last 18 sts, k2, yo, k1, yo, k2, p5, k1, sl 2tog k-wise, k1, p2sso, k1, p3 (221 sts).
Row 24: K3, (p3, k5, p7, k5) to last 18 sts, p3, k5, p7, k3.
Row 25: P3, (k2, sl 2tog k-wise, k1, p2sso, k2, p5, sl 2tog k-wise, k1, p2sso, p5) to last 18 sts, k2, sl 2tog k-wise, k1, p2sso, k2, p5, sl 2tog k-wise, k1, p2sso, p3 (177 sts).
Row 26: K3, (p1, k5, p5, k5) to last 18 sts, p1, k5, p5, k3.
Row 27: P3, (k1, sl 2tog k-wise, k1, p2sso, k1, p5, yo, k1, yo, p5) to last 18 sts, k1, sl 2tog k-wise, k1, p2sso, k1, p5, yo, k1, yo, p3.

Row 28: P3, (sl 2tog k-wise, k1, p2sso, p5, k1, yo, k1, yo,k1, p5) to last 18 sts, sl 2tog k-wise, k1, p2sso, p5, k1, yo, k1, yo, k1, p3.

Row 29: K3, (p5, k5, p1, k5) to last 14 sts, p5, k5, p1, k3.

Row 30: P3, (yo, k1, yo, p5, k2, yo, k1, yo, k2, p5) to last 14 sts, yo, k1, yo, p5, k2, yo, k1, yo, k2, p3 (221 sts).

Row 31: K3, (p7, k5, p3, k5) to last 18 sts, p7, k5, p3, k3.

Row 32: P3, (k1, yo, k1, yo, k1, p5, k2, sl 2tog k-wise, k1, p2sso, k2, p5) to last 18 sts, k1, yo, k1, yo, k1, p5, k2, sl 2tog k-wise, k1, p2sso, k2, p3.

Row 33: K3, (p5, k5) to last 8 sts, p5, k3.

Row 34: P3, (k2, yo, k1, yo, k2, p5, k1, sl 2tog k-wise, k1, p2sso, k1, p5) to last 18 sts, k2, yo, k1, yo, k2, p5, k1, sl 2tog k-wise, k1, p2sso, k1, p3.

Row 35: K3, (p3, k5, p7, k5) to last 18 sts, p3, k5, p7, k3.

Row 36: P3, (k2, sl 2tog k-wise, k1, p2sso, k2, p5, sl 2tog k-wise, k1, p2sso, p5) to last 18 sts, k2, sl 2tog k-wise, k1, p2sso, k2, p5, sl 2tog k-wise, k2, p2sso, p3) (177 sts).

Row 37: K3, (p1, k5, p5, k5) to last 14 sts, p1, k5, p5, k3.

Shape crown

Row 38 (dec): P3, (k1, sl 2tog k-wise, k1, p2sso, k1, p3, p2tog, k1, p2tog, p3) to last 14 sts, k1, sl 2tog k-wise, k1, p2sso, k1, p3, p2tog, k1, p2tog, p1 (133 sts).

Row 39: K2, (p1, k4, p3, k4) to last 10 sts, p1, k4, p3, k3.

Row 40: P3, (sl 2tog k-wise, k1, p2sso, p4, yo, k1, yo, p4) to last 10 sts, sl 2tog k-wise, k1, p2sso, p4, yo, k1, yo, p2.

Row 41: K2, (p3, k4, p1, k4), to last 11 sts, p3, k4, p1, k3.

Row 42: P1, (p2tog, k1, p2tog, p2, k1, yo, k1, yo, k1, p2) to end.

Row 43: K2, (p5, k3, p1, k3) to last 11 sts, p5, k3, p1, k2.

Row 44: P2, (yo, k1, yo, p3, k1, sl 2tog k-wise, k1, p2sso, k1, p3), to last 11 sts, yo, k1, yo, p3, k1, sl 2tog k-wise, k1, p2sso, k1, p2.

Row 45: K2, (p3, k3) to last 5 sts, p3, k2.

Row 46: P2, (k1, yo, k1, yo, k1, p3, sl 2tog k-wise, k1, p2sso, p3) to last 11 sts, k1, yo, k1, yo, k1, p3, sl 2tog k-wise, k1, p2sso, p2.

Row 47: K2, (p1, k3, p5, k3) to last 11 sts, p1, k3, p5, k2.

Row 48 (dec): P2, (k1, sl 2tog k-wise, k1, p2sso, k1, p1, p2tog, k1, p2tog, p1) to last 11 sts, k1, sl 2tog k-wise, k1, p2sso, k1, p1, p2tog, k1, p2tog (89 sts).

Row 49: K1, (p1, k2, p3, k2) to end.

Row 50 (dec): P2tog, (sl 2tog k-wise, k1, p2sso, p2tog, k1, p2tog) to last 7 sts, sl 2tog k-wise, k1, p2sso, p2tog, k1, p1 (45 sts).

Row 51: (K1, p1) to last st, k1.

Row 52: (p1, k1) to last st, p1.

Row 53 (dec): P1, (sl1 k-wise, k1, psso, p2tog) to end (23 sts).

Row 54: (k1, p1) to last st, k1.
Break yarn and thread through remaining 23 sts. Draw up tightly and fasten off.

Making up

Join the seam with a flat stitch.
Sew in ends.

The fabulous floral finisher on this cloche will give your day a rosy glow whenever you wear it. The hat is worked simply in double crochet, and a cord winds through a row of eyelets for added style.

Rosy cloche

Size

One size fits most

Actual measurements

21¼in (54cm) circumference at bottom edge, 8¾in (22cm) height

Materials

Rico Essentials Merino DK 100% extra fine superwash merino wool (131yds/120m per 50g ball):

2 balls in 03 Purple (A)

1 ball in 10 Magenta (B)

1 ball in 39 Petrol (C)

4mm (UK8:USG/6) crochet hook

Darning needle

Safety pin

Tension

22 sts and 11 rounds to 4in (10cm) over dc using 4mm hook.
Use larger or smaller hook if necessary to obtain correct tension.

Special abbreviations

Dc2inc: 2dc into next stitch (to increase).

Method

The cloche hat is worked in continuous rounds of double crochet with a row of half treble and chain stitches used to form eyelets just above the brim.

A crocheted cord is threaded through the eyelets and the hat is finished with a pretty rose corsage.

Hat

Using A, wind yarn around finger a couple of times to form a ring.

Round 1: Work 12 dc into ring. Pull on the short end of yarn to tighten the ring.

Round 2: (Dc2inc, 1 dc) 6 times (18 sts).

Round 3: (Dc2inc, 2 dc) 6 times (24 sts).

Round 4: (Dc2inc, 3 dc) 6 times (30 sts).

Round 5: (Dc2inc, 4 dc) 6 times (36 sts).

Round 6: (Dc2inc, 5 dc) 6 times (42 sts).

Round 7: (Dc2inc, 6 dc) 6 times (48 sts).

Round 8: (Dc2inc, 7 dc) 6 times (54 sts).

Round 9: (Dc2inc, 8 dc) 6 times (60 sts).

Round 10: (Dc2inc, 9 dc) 6 times (66 sts).

Round 11: (Dc2inc, 10 dc) 6 times (72 sts).

Round 12: (Dc2inc, 11 dc) 6 times (78 sts).

Round 13: (Dc2inc, 12 dc) 6 times (84 sts).

Round 14: (Dc2inc, 13 dc) 6 times (90 sts).

Round 15: (Dc2inc, 14 dc) 6 times (96 sts).

Round 16: (Dc2inc, 15 dc) 6 times (102 sts).

Round 17: (Dc2inc, 16 dc) 6 times (108 sts).

Round 18: (Dc2inc, 17 dc) 6 times (114 sts).

Rounds 19–42: Work even in dc.

Round 43: Make 2 ch, (skip next st, 1 htr, 1 ch) 56 times, ss to next 1 ch sp (57 ch sp).

Round 44: 2 dc into same 1 ch space as ss, 3 dc into next 1 ch sp, 2 dc into next 1 ch sp, (2 dc into next 1 ch sp, 3 dc into next 1 ch sp, 2 dc into next 1 ch sp) 18 times (133 sts).

Rounds 45–46: Work even in dc.

Round 47: (Dc2inc, 6 dc) 19 times (152 sts).

Rounds 48–52: Work even in dc.

Next round: Ss into the outside loops of each st. Fasten off and sew in ends.

Rose

Using B, leave a long length of yarn at beginning and make 39 ch.

Row 1: Work 1 tr into 4th ch from hook, 1 tr into each of next 35 ch, turn (36 sts).

Row 2: Make 4 ch, dtr4inc, (dtr5inc) to end. Fasten off leaving a long length of yarn at the end.

Leaf

Using C, make 16 ch.

Round 1: 1 dc into 2nd ch from hook, 1 dc into next 13 ch, 3 dc into end ch, 1 dc into other side of each ch to end (31 sts).

Round 2: Make 2 ch, 1 dc into first st of previous round, 1 dc, * (1 htr) twice, 1 tr, (1 dtr) 5 times, 1 tr, (1 htr) twice*, (1 dc) 5 times. Rep from * to *, (1 dc) twice, ss to next st, fasten off leaving a long length of yarn.

Cord

Using 4mm hook and B, make a chain measuring 45¼in (115cm).

Next row: Ss into 2nd ch from hook, ss to end. Fasten off and sew in ends.

Making up

With a large needle or safety pin, weave the cord in and out of the eyelets around the hat. Tie knots in each end of the cord and finish with a bow. Coil the narrow edge of the rose anti-clockwise, starting at the beginning of row 1, and use the long end of yarn to stitch as you go. Fasten off. Catch the long end of the yarn left from row 2 and thread it through the centre of the rose, then stitch the flower and leaves in place on the hat.

This design is inspired by moss-covered tree bark and
the rich colours of the natural landscape. It is highly textural
and a knitted rosette finishes off the top with a flourish.

Woodland

Size

One size fits most

Actual measurements

19in (48cm) circumference, 7in (18cm) height

Materials

Debbie Bliss Donegal Luxury Tweed Aran 85% wool, 15%
angora (96yds/88m per 50g ball):

1 ball in 29 Sienna (A)

1 ball in 25 Leaf (B)

A pair each of 4.5mm (UK7:US7) and 5mm (UK6:US8)
needles

Darning needle

Tension

18 sts and 30 rows to 4in (10cm) over pattern using 5mm needles. Use larger or smaller needles if necessary to obtain correct tension.

Method

This project starts with a few rows of garter stitch. The scallop design is created by increasing and decreasing, working with two colours, and reversing stocking stitch. The garter stitch decoration that tops the hat is worked by increasing the stitches on alternate rows, making a piece that curls naturally.

Hat

Using 4.5mm needles and A, cast on 82 sts.

Work 1¼in (3cm) in garter st.

Next row (inc): (K2, k twice in next st) 27 times, k1 (109 sts).

Change to 5mm needles and continue in patt:

Row 1 (RS): K1, *yf, k1, sl 1, k1, psso, k2, k2tog, k1, yf, k1, rep from * to end.

Row 2: With A, p to end.

Row 3: With A, rep row 1.

Rows 4 and 5: With B, p to end.

Row 6: With B, k to end.

Row 7: With B, rep row 1.

Rows 8–25: Rep rows 2 through 7 three times.

Row 26 (dec): With A, p4, (p2tog, p7) to last 6 sts, p2tog, p4 (97 sts).

Row 27: With A, K1, *yf, k1, sl 1, k1, psso, k1, k2tog, k1, yf, k1, rep from * to end.

Rows 28 and 29: With B, p to end.

Row 30: With B, k to end.

Row 31: With B, K1, *yf, k1, sl 1, k1, psso, k1, k2tog, k1, yf, k1, rep from * to end.

Row 32: With A, p to end.

Row 33 (dec): With A, k1, *yf, k1, sl 2 k-wise, k1, p2sso, k2tog, k1, yf, k1, rep from * to end (85 sts).

Rows 34 and 35: With B, p to end.

Row 36: With B, k to end.

Row 37: With B, k1, *yf, k1, sl 1, k1, psso, k2tog, k1, yf, k1, rep from * to end.

Row 38: With A, p to end.

Row 39: With A, k1, *yf, k1, sl 1, k1, psso, k2tog, k1, yf, k1, rep from * to end.

Row 40 (dec): With B, p3, (p2tog, p5) to last 5 sts, p2tog, p3 (73 sts).

Rows 41 and 42: With B, p to end.

Row 43: With B, k1, *yf, k1, sl 2 k-wise, k1, p2sso, k1, yf, k1, rep from * to end.

Row 44: With A, p to end.

Row 45 (dec): With A, k2, *sl 2tog k-wise, k1, p2sso, k3, rep from * to last 5 sts, sl 2tog k-wise, k1, p2sso, k2 (49 sts).

Row 46: With B, p to end.

Row 47 (dec): With B, p1, (p2tog, p1) to end (33 sts).

Row 48: With B, k to end.

Break yarn and thread through remaining 33 sts. Draw up tightly and fasten off.

Decoration

Leaving a long length of yarn and with 5mm needles and A, cast on 30 sts.

Row 1 and every alt row: Knit.

Row 2 (inc): (K twice in each st) 30 times (60 sts).

Row 4 (inc): (K1, k twice in next st) 30 times (90 sts).

Row 6 (inc): (K1, k twice in next st) 45 times (135 sts).

Rows 8–10: With yarn B, k to end. Cast off. Stretch the cast-off edge, then coil the piece round and stitch in place along the base.

Making up

Sew back seam with a flat stitch, carefully matching the pattern. Attach the finished decoration to the top of the hat.

This elegant vintage-style hat with a decorative buckle will dress up an outfit for a cool evening. You can use a retro-style buckle or have a go at tracking down the genuine article for an authentic look.

Bonny

Size

One size fits most

Actual measurements

19in (48cm) circumference, 7½in (19cm) height

Materials

Rico Essentials Merino DK 100% extra fine superwash merino wool (131yds/120m per 50g ball):

2 balls in 60 Cream

A pair each of 3.25mm (UK10:US3) and 4mm (UK8:US6) knitting needles

Darning needle

Vintage or retro-style buckle

Tension

20 sts and 26 rows to 4in (10cm) over st st using 4mm needles. Use larger or smaller needles if necessary to obtain correct tension.

Method

The main part of the hat is knitted with a moss stitch edge and continued in stocking stitch. The band is knitted separately in moss stitch. After adding the buckle, the band is stitched in place on the hat at the centre front and centre back, leaving the edges free so the wearer can adjust its position.

Hat

Using 3.25mm needles, cast on 112 sts.
Row 1 (RS): (K1, p1) to end.
Row 2: (P1, k1) to end.
These 2 rows form the moss st pattern. Work ¾in (2cm) in moss st ending, with a WS row.
Change to 4mm needles and continue in st st until work measures 6¼in (16cm) from cast-on edge.

Shape crown

Row 1 (dec): (K2, k2tog) to end (84 sts).
Work 3 rows.
Row 5 (dec): (K1, k2tog) to end (56 sts).
Work 3 rows.
Row 9 (dec): (K2tog) to end (28 sts).
Work 3 rows.
Break yarn and thread through remaining 28 sts. Draw up tightly and fasten off.

Band

With 4mm needles, cast on 112 sts and work in moss st for 3½in (9cm). Cast off in moss st.

Making up

Join the back seam of the hat. Thread the band through the buckle so it sits at the centre front. Use a flat stitch to sew the centre back seam of the band. Position the band with the seam matching the seam of the hat and stitch through both seams to join. Make a few stitches at the centre front, through the band in the middle of the buckle and into the hat, to hold both the band and the buckle in place.

Some clever stitchery makes this bold pattern with twisted stripes. And it's a lot easier than it looks – you only need to work one colour per row. The hat is worked flat and then seamed up the back.

Barley-twist stripes

Size

One size fits most

Actual measurements

18⅞in (48cm) circumference, 8in (20.5cm) height

Materials

Rico Essentials Merino DK 100% extra fine superwash merino wool (131yds/120m per 50g ball):

1 ball in 05 Red (A)

1 ball in 27 Jeans (B)

A pair each of 3.25mm (UK10:US3) and 4mm (UK8:US6) knitting needles

Darning needle

Tension

20 sts and 26 rows to 4in (10cm) over st st using 4mm needles. Use larger or smaller needles if necessary to obtain correct tension.

Special abbreviations

m3: Knit into front, back then front again of next stitch.

Method

After starting with a 1 x 1 rib, the vertical stripes are formed by using one colour for each row and slipping alternate stitches. The pattern is created by knitting three times into one stitch and working into those extra stitches for a couple of rows. Then the three are worked together again to make one stitch and the process is repeated. The hat is completed in a block of one-colour stocking stitch and topped with a red tassel.

Hat

Using 3.25mm needles and A, cast on 113 sts.

Work in k1, p1 rib for 1¼in (3cm). Change to 4mm needles and work in patt as follows:

Next row (WS): P1, *p1 winding yarn 3 times around the needle, p1. Rep from * to end.

Row 1 (RS): With B, m3, *with yarn at back sl 1 letting the extra loops drop, m3 in next st. Rep from * to end.

Row 2: With B, p3, *with yarn at front, sl 1, p3. Rep from * to end.

Row 3: With B, k3, *sl 1, k3. Rep from * to end.

Row 4: With B, p3tog, *sl 1, p3tog winding yarn twice around the needle. Rep from * to last 4 sts, sl 1, p3tog.

Row 5: With A, k1, *m3, sl 1 letting extra loops drop. Rep from * to last 2 sts, m3, k1.

Row 6: With A, k1, *p3, sl 1. Rep from * to last 4 sts, p3, k1.

Row 7: With A, k1, *k3, sl 1. Rep from * to last 4 sts, k4.

Row 8: With A, k1, *p3tog winding yarn twice around the needle, sl 1. Rep from * to last 4 sts, p3tog winding yarn twice around the needle, k1.

These 8 rows form the pattern. Rep the pattern 3 more times, then work rows 1 through 7 again.

Row 40: With A, k1, *p3tog, sl 1. Rep from * to last 4 sts, p3tog, k1.

Continue with B in st st, starting with a k row, until work measures 5½in (14cm) from cast-on edge.

Shape crown

Row 1 (dec): K3, (k2tog, k5) to last 5 sts, k2tog, k3 (97 sts).

Work 3 rows.

Row 5 (dec): K3, (k2tog, k4) to last 4 sts, k2tog, k2 (81 sts).

Work 3 rows.

Row 9 (dec): K3, (k2tog, k3) to last 3 sts, k3tog (64 sts).

Work 3 rows.

Row 13 (dec): (K2, k2tog) to end (48 sts).

Work 3 rows.

Row 17 (dec): (K1, k2tog) to end (32 sts).

Work 1 row.

Break yarn and thread through remaining 32 sts. Draw up tightly and fasten off.

Making up

Join the back seam carefully matching the pattern. Make a tassel (see page 152) in A and attach it to the top of the hat.

Fend off any gusts of wind with this hooded scarf to protect both head and neck. The piece is simply worked in a rib pattern and embellished with a full fringe at either end.

Hooded scarf

Size

One size fits most

Actual measurements

41in (104cm) from top of hood to end of scarf, excluding fringe

Materials

Rowan Kid Classic 70% lambswool, 26% kid mohair, 4% nylon (153yds/140m per 50g ball):

4 balls in 852 Victoria

A pair of 5.5mm (UK5:US9) needles

Darning needle

Crochet hook

Cardboard for making fringe

Tension

30 sts and 22 rows to 4in (10cm) over rib pattern, without stretching. Use larger or smaller needles if necessary to obtain correct tension.

Method

The hooded scarf is knitted in one long piece of 2 x 2 rib that is shaped at the back, from the neck to the top of the head, and stitched at the seam. A fringe of tassels is added to each end of the scarf.

Scarf and hood

Cast on 54 sts.

Row 1 (RS): *K2, p2; rep from * to last 2 sts, k2.

Row 2 (WS): *P2, k2; rep from * to last 2 sts, p2.

Repeat these 2 rows forming the rib pattern until work measures 29½in (75cm) ending with WS row.

Shape hood

Keeping in patt as set, inc 1 st at beg of next row and every following alt row until there are 64 sts, then every 4th row until there are 70 sts.

Work 40 rows without shaping, ending with a WS row.

Next row (RS): Dec 1 st at beg of this row and every 4th row until there are 64 sts, then every alternate row until there are 54 sts.

Continue in k2, p2 rib until work measures 29½in (75cm) from end of hood shaping.

Cast off loosely in rib pattern.

Making up

Fold the work in half lengthwise so that it measures 41in (104cm) and sew the back seam from beg of shaping to the folded top edge.

Fringe

Cut a piece of cardboard 6in (15cm) long and wind the yarn around it 7 times. Cut through one edge of yarn. Insert the crochet hook from the WS to the RS of the work, fold the yarn in half and draw through. Now draw the cut ends through the loop to tighten. Trim ends.

Make 14 tassels for each end and attach them evenly across the end (see page 152 for details).

Trapper hats are very trendy at the moment and this fur-effect one looks like the real deal. With its cozy earflaps this is all you need to stay warm and look cool.

Furry trapper

Size

One size fits most women [one size fits most men]

Actual measurements

22¾in/58cm [23½in/60cm] circumference

Materials

Sirdar Tweedie Chunky 45% acrylic, 40% wool, 15% alpaca (108yds/100m per 50g ball):
2 balls in 281 Truffle (A)
Sirdar Funky Fir 100% polyester (98yds/90m per 50g ball):
1 ball in 549 Walnut (B)
A pair each of 5mm (UK6:US8) and 6mm (UK4:US10) needles
A set of 5mm (UK6:US8) double-pointed needles

Tension

12 sts and 20 rows to 4in (10cm) over st st using 6mm needles and A.

Method

The earflaps are knitted first, then stitches are cast on between them to form a back panel. The middle band and crown are knitted separately, then the three pieces are joined together. Fur linings are then knitted for the earflaps, back panel and front band and sewn in place.

Hat

Left earflap

Using 6mm needles and A cast on 3 sts.

Row 1 (RS): Inc 1, k1, inc 1 (5 sts).
Row 2: K2, p1, k2.
Row 3: K2, m1, k1, m1, k2 (7 sts).
Row 4 and foll alternate rows through 12: K2, purl to last 2 sts, k2.
Row 5: K2, m1, k3, m1, k2 (9 sts).
Row 7: K2, m1, k5, m1, k2 (11 sts).
Row 9: K2, m1, k7, m1, k2 (13 sts).
Row 11: Knit.
Row 13: Knit.
Row 14: K2, purl to last 2 sts, k2.
Row 15: K2, m1, knit to end (14 sts).
Row 16: K2, purl to last 2 sts, m1, k2 (15 sts).

Row 17: K2, m1, knit to end (16 sts).
Row 18: K2, purl to last 2 sts, m1, k2 (17 sts).
Leave sts on a length of yarn or a stitch holder.

Right earflap

Work as left earflap from through row 14.
Row 15: Knit to last 2 sts, m1, k2. (14 sts).
Row 16: k2, m1, p to last 2 sts, k2 (15 sts).
Row 17: Knit to last 2 sts, m1, k2 (16 sts).
Row 18: k2, m1, p to last 2 sts, k2 (17 sts).

Back neck panel

With right side facing and using 6mm needles and yarn A, knit 17 sts of right earflap, cast on 16 [18] sts, knit 17 sts of left earflap (50 [52] sts).
Row 1 (WS): K2, p13, k2, k16 (18), k2, p13, k2.
Row 2: Knit.
Row 3: K2, purl to last 2 sts, k2.
Row 4: Knit.
Rep rows 3 and 4 two [three] times, then rep row 3 once.
Cast off loosely.

Middle band

Using 6mm needles and yarn A cast on 15 [17] sts.
Row 1 (RS): Knit.
Row 2: K3, purl to last 3 sts, k3.
Rep rows 1 and 2 until the band is of sufficient length to fit around the head (approx. 22¾in/58cm for woman's size, 23½in/60cm for man's size). Cast off.

Circular crown

Using 5mm needles and A cast on 3 sts.
Next row: Increase in every st (6 sts).
Divide these sts on to 3 double pointed 5mm needles (2 sts on each needle). Mark the start of each round with a loop of yarn or stitch marker.
Round 1: Inc in every st (12 sts).
Round 2: *Inc1, k1, inc1, k1; rep from * to end of round (18 sts).
Round 3: *Inc1, k2, inc1, k2; rep from * to end of round (24 sts).
Round 4: *Inc1, k3, inc1, k3; rep from * to end of round (30 sts).
Round 5: *Inc1, k4, inc1, k4; rep from * to end of round (36 sts).
Round 6: *Inc1, k5, inc1, k5; rep from * to end of round (42 sts).
Round 7: *Inc1, k6, inc1, k6; rep from * to end of round (48 sts).
Round 8: *Inc1, k7, inc1, k7; rep from * to end of round (54 sts).
Round 9: *Inc1, k8, inc1, k8; rep from * to end of round (60 sts).

Round 10: *Inc1, k9, inc1, k9; rep from * to end of round (66 sts).

Round 11: *Inc1, k10, inc1, k10; rep from * to end of round (72 sts).

Round 12: *Inc1, k11, inc1, k11; rep from * to end of round (78 sts).

Round 13: *Inc1, k12, inc1, k12; rep from * to end of round (84 sts).

Round 14: *Inc1, k13, inc1, k13; rep from * to end of round (90 sts).

Round 15 (second size only): Inc1, k14, Inc1, k14 (96 sts).

Work 1 round without shaping.

Next round (both sizes): Inc1, k14 [15], Inc1, k14 [15] (96 [102] sts).

Work 1 round without shaping.

Cast off.

Making up

Sew the cast-on and cast-off edges of the middle band together using mattress stitch.

Join the middle band to the earflaps section using mattress stitch (placing seam of middle band at back).

Attach the circular crown to the top of the middle panel, easing to fit as required.

Furry linings
Front band lining

Using 5mm needles and B cast on 12 [14] sts. Work in st st until band measures approx. 7½in (19cm). Cast off.

Earflaps and back neck panel lining
Left earflap

Using 5mm needles and B cast on 3 sts

Row 1: Inc 1, k1, inc 1 (5sts).

Row 2 and foll alternate rows: Purl.

Row 3: K2, m1, k1, m1, k2 (7sts).

Row 5: K2, m1, k3, m1, k2 (9sts).

Row 7: K2, m1, k5, m1, k2 (11sts).

Row 9: K2, m1, k7, m1, k2 (13sts).

Row 11: K2, m1, k9, m1, k2 (15sts).

Row 12: Purl.

Row 13: Knit.

Row 14: Purl.

Rows 15–20: Rep rows 13 and 14.

Row 21: K1, m1, knit to end (16sts).

Row 22 and foll alternate rows: Purl.

Row 23: K1, m1, knit to end (17sts).

Row 25: K1, m1, knit to end (18sts).

Row 27: K1, m1, knit to end.(19sts).

Row 28: Purl.

Leave sts on a length of yarn or a stitch holder.

Right earflap

Work as left earflap from through row 20.

Row 21: Knit to last st, m1, k1 (16 sts).

Row 22 and foll alternate rows: Purl

Row 23: Knit to last st, m1, k1 (17 sts).

Row 25: Knit to last st, m1, k1 (18 sts).

Row 27: Knit to last st, m1, k1 (19 sts).

Row 28: Purl.

Back neck panel

With right side facing and using B knit 19 sts of right earflap, cast on 16 [18] sts, knit 19 sts of left earflap (54 [56] sts).

Work 9 rows in st st.

Cast off loosely.

Making up

With WS together sew the earflaps/back panel lining inside the outer helmet, easing to fit and using a loose slip stitch – the lining should slightly overlap at the lower edges of the helmet and earflaps so it can be seen from the right side.

Lay the front fur band on top of the front middle band between the two earflaps (RS facing outwards for both) and slip stitch in place.

Quick and easy to make, this crocheted cap has a bold and eye-catching design worked in contrasting colours. The triangles are made up of a simple combination of trebles and chains.

Chunky cutie

Size

One size fits most

Actual measurements

19½in (50cm) circumference, 8in (20cm) height

Materials

Rowan Big Wool 100% merino wool (87yds/80m per 100g ball):

1 ball in 007 Smoky (A)

1 ball in 048 Linen (B)

12mm (UK-:USO/16) crochet hook

Darning needle

Tension

8 sts and 6 rounds to 4in (10cm) over dc using 12mm hook.

Use larger or smaller hook if necessary to obtain correct tension.

Method

The crown of the hat is worked in alternate coloured stripes of double crochet, then a round of triangular stitches is created by working one treble behind the first, with a chain space in between, followed by a round of double crochet. These two rounds are repeated until the hat reaches the required length.

Special abbreviations

Dc2inc: 2 dc into next stitch (to increase).

Hat

With A, make 4 ch and ss to first ch to form a ring.

Round 1: 1 ch (does not count as a st). Work 6 dc into the ring, ss to next st.

Round 2 (inc): (Dc2inc in next st) 6 times (12 sts), ss to next st.

Round 3 (inc): Join in B, (dc2inc, 1 dc) 6 times (18 sts), ss to next st.

Round 4 (inc): With A, (dc2inc, 2 dc) 6 times (24 sts), ss to next st.

Round 5 (inc): With B, (dc2inc, 3 dc) 6 times (30 sts), ss to next st.

Round 6: With A, work 1 dc into each st to end, ss to next st.

Round 7: With B, make 3 ch (to count as tr), 1 tr into the dc behind the 3 ch just worked, (1 ch, skip 2 dc, 1 tr into next dc, 1 tr into the 2nd skipped dc, behind the tr just worked) 9 times, 1 ch, ss to 3rd of 3 ch.

Round 8: With A, work 1 dc into each st and 1 ch sp to end, ss to next st.

Round 9: With B, ss into next st, 3 ch (to count as tr), 1 tr into the dc behind the ss and 3 ch just worked, (1 ch, skip 2 dc, 1 tr into next dc, 1 tr into the 2nd skipped dc, behind the tr just worked) 9 times, 1 ch, ss to 3rd of 3 ch.

Round 10: As round 8.
Round 11: As round 9.
Round 12: As round 8. Fasten off.

Finishing

Sew in yarn ends.

The pheasant feathers that decorate this hat may well be mistaken at first glance for those picked up along a country path. The brim is worked with a picot edge.

Country feathers

Size

One size fits most

Actual measurements

19½in (50cm) circumference, above the brim

Materials

BC Garn Allino 50% cotton, 50% linen (137yds/125m per 50g ball):

2 balls in 01 Deep Brown (A)

1 ball in 02 Acorn (B)

1 ball in 03 Taupe (C)

A pair each of 3mm (UK11:US-) and 3.25mm (UK10:US3) needles

Darning needle

Tension

24 sts and 30 rows to 4in (10cm) over st st using 3.25mm needles. Use larger or smaller needles if necessary to obtain correct tension.

Method

The crown is knitted first in stocking stitch, then the cast-on stitches of the crown are picked up, knitted and increased to shape the brim. Eyelets are worked into one of the last few rows of the brim which, when turned under, form a picot edge. Feathers are worked in three shades of brown and stitched in place after making up the hat.

Hat

Using 3.25mm needles and A, cast on 120 sts and work 5½in (14cm) in st st.

Shape crown

Row 1 (dec): (K6, k2tog) 15 times (105 sts).
Row 2: Purl.
Row 3 (dec): (K5, k2tog) 15 times (90 sts).
Row 4: Purl.
Row 5 (dec): (K4, k2tog) 15 times (75 sts).
Row 6: Purl.
Row 7 (dec): (K3, k2tog) 15 times (60 sts).
Row 8: Purl.

Row 9 (dec): (K2, k2tog) 15 times (45 sts).
Row 10: Purl.
Row 11 (dec): (K1, k2tog) 15 times (30 sts).
Row 12: Purl.
Row 13 (dec): (K2tog) 15 times (15 sts).
Break yarn and thread through remaining 15 sts. Draw up tightly and fasten off.

Brim

With RS of work facing, pick up and knit 120 sts from the cast-on edge.
Row 1: Purl.
Row 2 (inc): (K3, k twice in next st) 30 times (150 sts).
Rows 3–5: Beg with a purl row, work 3 rows in st st.
Row 6 (inc): (K4, k twice in next st) 30 times (180 sts).
Rows 7–17: Beg with a purl row, work 11 rows in st st.

Picot edge

Row 18: K1, (yf, k2tog) to last st, k1.
Row 19: Purl.
Rows 20–23: Beg with a knit row, work 4 rows in st st.
Cast off.

Large feather

With 3mm needles and B, cast on 3 sts.
Row 1 and every alt row (WS): Purl with the colour used on previous row.
Row 2 (inc): K1, yf, k1, yf, k1 (5 sts).
Row 4 (inc): Join C, k2, yf, k1, yf, k2 (7 sts).
Row 6 (inc): Join A, k3, yf, k1, yf, k3 (9 sts).
Row 8 (inc): With C, k4, yf, k1, yf, k4 (11 sts).
Row 10 (inc): With B, k5, yf, k1, yf, k5 (13 sts).
Row 12 (inc): K6, yf, k1, yf, k6 (15 sts).
Row 14 (inc): With C, k7, yf, k1, yf, k7 (17 sts).
Row 16: With A, k7, yf, sl 2, k1, p2sso, yf, k7.
Row 18: With C, k7, yf, sl 2, k1, p2sso, yf, k7.
Row 20: With B, k7, yf, sl 2, k1, p2sso, yf, k7.
Row 22: As row 20.
Row 24 (dec): With C, k7, sl 2, k1, p2sso, k7 (15 sts).
Row 26: With A, k6, yf, sl 2, k1, yf, k6.
Row 28 (dec): With C, k6, sl 2, k1, p2sso, k6 (13 sts).
Row 30: With B, K5, yf, sl 2, k1, yf, k5.
Row 32 (dec): K5, sl 2, k1, p2sso, k5 (11 sts).

Row 34: With C, k4, yf, sl 2, k1, p2sso, yf, k4.

Row 36 (dec): With A, k4, sl 2, k1, p2sso, k4 (9 sts).

Row 38: With C, k3, yf, sl 2, k1, p2sso, yf, k3.

Row 40 (dec): With B, k3, sl 2, k1, p2sso, k3 (7 sts).

Row 42: With B, k2, yf, sl 2, k1, p2sso, yf, k2.

Row 44 (dec): With C, k2, sl 2, k1, p2sso, k2 (5 sts).

Row 46: With A, k1, yf, sl 2, k1, p2sso, yf, k1.

Row 48 (dec): With C, k1, sl 2, k1, p2sso, k1 (3 sts).

Row 50: Sl 2, k1, p2sso (1 st).
Fasten off.

Small feather

With 3mm needles and B, cast on 3 sts and work as for large feather from rows 1 through 11, then work as rows 30 through 50.

Making up

Stitch the back seam. Turn under the brim at the eyelet row to form picots and slip stitch in place. Position feathers on the hat as shown in the image and sew along the centre of each, leaving the edges free to curl under naturally.

Tri-coloured yarn coupled with a bobbly pattern make a wonderfully textured pattern. Knitted with a wool and alpaca blend, the hat's as pretty as it is warm.

Bobbly beanie

Size
One size fits most
Actual measurements
19½in (50cm) circumference

Materials
Adriafil Lana Naturale Inca 50% alpaca, 50% wool
(110yds/100m per 50g ball):
2 balls in 72 Moulinet Beige/Grey
4.5mm (UK7:US7) crochet hook
Darning needle

Tension

14 sts and 8 rounds to 4in (10cm) over pattern using 4.5mm hook. Use larger or smaller hook if necessary to obtain correct tension.

Method

This hat is crocheted in rounds of treble stitches with clusters of trebles worked in to form the bobbly pattern. A slightly bulkier cluster of trebles lines the rim of the hat with a round of double crochet to finish it off.

Special abbreviations

Bobble: (Yrh, insert hook into st, yrh, draw back through stitch) 4 times in same st, yrh, draw through 8 loops on hook, yrh, draw through last 2 loops.

Tr2inc: 2 tr into next stitch (to increase).

Tr2dec: Yrh, insert hook into next st, yrh draw back through st, yrh draw through 2 sts on hook (2 sts left on hook), yrh, insert hook into next st, yrh, draw back through st (4 loops on hook), yrh, draw through 2 loops on hook, yrh, draw through remaining 3 loops (to decrease).

Hat

Using 4.5mm hook, work 4 ch and join with ss to form a ring.

Round 1 (inc): 3 ch (counts as first tr), 14 tr into ring, ss to top of 3 ch (15 sts).

Round 2 (inc): 3 ch, 1 tr in same st as 3 ch was worked, tr2inc, *(make bobble, 1 tr) in next st, tr2inc, (1 tr, make bobble) in next st, (tr2inc) twice. Rep from * twice, (make bobble, 1 tr) in next st, tr2inc, (1 tr, make bobble) in next st, ss to top of 3 ch (30 sts).

Round 3 (inc): 3 ch, (tr2inc, 1 tr in next st) 14 times, tr2inc, ss to top of 3 ch (45 sts).

Round 4 (inc): 3 ch, 1 tr in next st, (tr2inc, 1 tr in next 2 sts) 14 times, tr2inc, ss to top of 3 ch (60 sts).

Round 5 (inc): 3 ch, 1 tr in same st as 3 ch was worked, (make bobble, 1 tr, tr2inc, 1 tr) 14 times, make bobble, 1 tr in next 2 sts, ss to top of 3 ch (75 sts).

Round 6 (inc): 3 ch, 1 tr in same st as 3 ch was worked, (1 tr in next 4 sts, tr2inc) 14 times, 1 tr in next 4 sts, ss to top of 3 ch (90 sts).

Round 7: 3 ch, 1 tr in each st, ss to top of 3 ch.

Round 8: 3 ch, 1 tr in next 3 sts, (make bobble, 1 tr in next 4 sts) 17 times, make bobble, ss to top of 3 ch.

Rounds 9–10: As round 7.

Rounds 11–13: Rep rounds 8 to 10 once more.

Round 14: As round 8.

Round 15 (dec): 3 ch, (tr2dec, 1 tr in next st) 29 times, tr2dec, ss to top of 3 ch (60 sts).

Round 16: 1 ch, *(yrh, insert hook into next st, yrh, draw back through st, yrh, draw through 2 loops on hook) 4 times in same st, yrh, draw through 5 loops on hook, 1 ch, 1 dc. Rep from * 30 times, omitting the last dc. Ss to 1 ch.

Round 17: Work 1 dc in each ch and dc to end. Ss to next st. Fasten off.

Finishing

Sew in ends. Shape hat, pushing bobbles outwards from the inside with a finger.

This delightful little parcel for your head knits up in a snap with chunky yarn and large needles. The cascading ribbon effect is created with mock cables.

Ribbons and bow

Size

One size fits most

Actual measurements

18⅞in (48cm) circumference, 7½in (19cm) height

Materials

Rowan Big Wool 100% merino wool (87yds/80m per 100g ball):

1 ball in 059 Oxidised

A pair of 10mm (UK000:US15) needles

Darning needle

Tension

9 sts and 14 rows to 4in (10cm) over pattern.

Use larger or smaller needles if necessary to obtain correct tension.

Method

The hat is knitted flat with mock cables and seamed up the back. The bow is knitted in two lengths of stocking stitch and sewn together.

Special abbreviations

T2b (Knitted crossed stitches with back twist): Pass the right-hand needle behind the first stitch on the left-hand needle, knit into the back of the second stitch and leave on the needle. Knit into the back of the first stitch and slip both stitches off the left-hand needle together.

Hat

Cast on 43 sts.

Row 1 (RS): P3, (k2, p3) to end.

Row 2: K3, (p2, k3) to end.

Rows 3 and 4: Rep rows 1 and 2.

Row 5: P3, (t2b, p3) to end.

Row 6: Rep row 2.

These 6 rows form the pattern. Rep pattern twice more.

Shape crown

Row 19 (RS): P2tog, p1, (k2, p2tog, p1) to end (34 sts).

Row 20: K2, (p2, k2) to end.

Row 21: P2tog, (k2, p2tog) to end (25 sts).

Row 22: K1, (p2, k1) to end.

Row 23: P1, (sl1, k1, psso, p1) to end (17 sts).

Row 24: K1, (p1, k1) to end.

Break yarn and thread through remaining 17 sts. Draw up and fasten off.

Bow

Cast on 7 sts.

Work in st st for 9in (23cm). Cast off.

Knot

Cast on 4 sts.

Work in st st for 2¾in (7cm). Cast off.

Making up

Join the back seam of hat. Fold the bow piece in half and stitch the short edges together. Position the seam at the centre back. Wrap the knot piece around the centre of the bow. Join the edges and stitch in place at the back. Sew in place on the hat.

Tip

It's up to you how you wear this hat. You can position the bow at the front, but it will look equally stylish with it at the side – or even the back.

Greta Garbo would have been proud to wear this turban knitted up in bold and rich red wool. Stocking and reverse stocking stitches are used to form the ridges.

Turban chic

Size

One size fits most

Actual measurements

21¼in (54cm) circumference at bottom edge

Materials

Jamieson & Smith 2ply Jumper Weight 100% Shetland wool (125yds/115m per 25g ball):

2 balls in 9097 Flamingo

A pair of 3.25mm (UK10:US3) needles

Darning needle

Tension

28 sts and 34 rows to 4in (10cm) over st st using 3.25mm needles.
Use larger or smaller needles if necessary to obtain correct tension.

Method

The turban is knitted in stocking stitch, which is reversed every few rows to create the effect of a gathered fabric. The hat is knitted in one piece, then stitched to form the finished shape.

Hat

Cast on 140 sts.
Work 4 rows in g st.
Continue in pattern as follows:

Row 1 (WS): Knit.
Row 2: Purl.
Rep last 2 rows 3 more times.
Row 9: Purl.
Row 10: Knit.
Rows 11–16: Rep last 2 rows 3 more times.
Rep rows 1–16 three more times.
Row 65: Knit.
Row 66: Purl.
Rep last 2 rows twice.
Row 71: Knit.
Row 72 (dec): (P2tog, p3) to end (112 sts).

Shape top

Row 1 (WS): K66, sl1 p-wise, turn.
Row 2: K21, sl 1 p-wise, turn.
Row 3: P22, sl 1 p-wise, turn.
Row 4: K23, sl 1 p-wise, turn.
Row 5: P24, sl 1 p-wise, turn.
Row 6: K25, sl 1 p-wise, turn.
Row 7: P26, sl 1 p-wise, turn.
Row 8: K27, sl 1 p-wise, turn.
Row 9: P28, sl 1 p-wise, turn.
Row 10: P29, sl 1 p-wise, turn.
Row 11: K30, sl 1 p-wise, turn.
Row 12: P31, sl 1 p-wise, turn.
Row 13: K32, sl 1 p-wise, turn.
Row 14: P33, sl 1 p-wise, turn.
Row 15: K34, sl 1 p-wise, turn.
Row 16: P35, sl 1 p-wise, turn.
Row 17: K36, sl 1 p-wise, turn.
Row 18: *K2tog, k35, sl 1 p-wise, turn (111 sts).
Row 19: P2tog, p35, sl 1 p-wise, turn (110 sts).
Rows 20–25: Rep last 2 rows 3 more times.
Row 26: P2tog, p35, sl 1 p-wise, turn (103 sts).
Row 27: K2tog, k35, sl 1 p-wise, turn (102 sts).
Rows 28–33: Rep last 2 rows 3 more times (96 sts).
Rep rows from * once more (80 sts).
Row 50: As row 18 (79 sts).
Row 51: As row 19 (78 sts).
Rep last 2 rows 3 more times (72 sts).
Row 58: As row 26 (71 sts).

Row 59: As row 27 (70 sts).
Row 60: P2tog, p33, p2tog, sl 1 p-wise, turn (68 sts).
Row 61: K2tog, k32, k2tog, sl 1 p-wise, turn (66 sts).
Row 62: P2tog, p31, p2tog, sl 1 p-wise, turn (64 sts).
Row 63: K2tog, k30, k2tog, sl 1 p-wise, turn (62 sts).
Row 64: P2tog, p29, p2tog, sl 1 p-wise, turn (60 sts).
Row 65: K2tog, k28, k2tog, sl 1 p-wise, turn (58 sts).
Row 66: K2tog, k27, k2tog, sl 1 p-wise, turn (56 sts).
Row 67: P2tog, p26, p2tog, sl 1 p-wise, turn (54 sts).
Row 68: K2tog, k25, k2tog, sl 1 p-wise, turn (52 sts).
Row 69: P2tog, p24, p2tog, sl 1 p-wise, turn (50 sts).
Row 70: K2tog, k23, k2tog, sl 1 p-wise, turn (48 sts).
Row 71: P2tog, p22, p2tog, sl 1 p-wise, turn (46 sts).
Row 72: K2tog, k21, k2tog, sl 1 p-wise, turn (44 sts).
Row 73: (P2tog) 12 times (32 sts). Leave the 10 sts from the left-hand needle on a spare needle, turn.
Row 74: K12, leave remaining 10 sts on a spare needle.
Continue on these 12 sts in g st for 4in (10cm). Cast off.
With RS facing, sl the rem 20 sts onto

the left-hand needle, so the side edges of the work meet.

Next row (RS): Rejoin yarn and (k2tog) 10 times, working across all sts. Cast off.

Making up

Turn under the 4 rows of garter stitch and slip stitch to the inside of the hat. Join the centre front seam, matching the pattern. Run gathering stitches down the seam and draw up to 2in (5cm). Fasten off. Turn the hat right side out and pull the garter stitch panel from the inside of the hat out and over the top to cover the gathered seam. Slip stitch the cast-off edge in place along the first row of garter stitch on the outside of the hat, covering the cast-off stitches across the top of the gathered centre front. Fasten off.

Tip
Wear with your hair down for a relaxed daytime look or tuck your hair up into the turban for a sophisticated evening style.

This project has all the elements of a classic peaked cap – crown, band and peak – and decorative buttons add the finishing touch. The cap is knitted flat and seamed up the back.

Peaked perfection

Size

One size fits most

Actual measurements

19½in (50cm) circumference (excluding brim)

Materials

Rowan Cocoon 80% merino wool, 20% kid mohair
(126yds/115m per 100g ball):
2 balls in 813 Seascape
A pair of 7mm (UK2:US-) needles
Darning needle
2 buttons

Tension

18 sts and 17 rows to 4in (10cm) over pattern using 7mm needles. Use larger or smaller needles if necessary to obtain correct tension.

Special abbreviations

T2f (Knitted crossed stitches with front twist): Pass the right needle in front of the first stitch on the left needle; knit the next stitch, leaving it on the needle; knit the first stitch and slip both stitches off the left needle together.

Method

The hat is knitted in a twisted stitch, and a patterned peak and strap are worked separately. The pieces are sewn together and two buttons are added to decorate.

Hat

Cast on 75 sts.

Set-up row: K8 (k twice in next st, k10) 6 times, k twice in last st (82 sts).

Row 1 (RS): P2, (t2f, p2) to end.

Row 2: K2, (p2, k2) to end.

These 2 rows form the pattern. Continue in pattern until work measures 6in (15.5cm), ending with row 1.

Shape crown

Row 1 (WS): (K2tog, p2) to last 2 sts, k2 tog (61 sts).

Row 2: P1, (t2f, p1) to end.

Row 3: P1, (p2tog, p1) to end (41 sts).

Row 4: (T2f) to last st, p1.

Row 5: (P2tog, p1) to last 2 sts, p2tog (27 sts).

Row 6: Knit.

Break yarn and thread through rem 27 sts. Draw up tightly and fasten off.

Peak

(make 2)

Cast on 37 sts.

Row 1 (WS): P2, (with yarn forward sl 1 p-wise, p1) to last st, p1.

Row 2: P2tog, p to last 2 sts, p2tog (35 sts).

Row 3: (P1, with yarn forward sl 1 p-wise) to last st, p1.

Row 4: P2tog, p to last 2 sts, p2 tog (33 sts).

Rep these 4 rows, decreasing at each end of every RS row, until there are 25 sts.

Cast off k-wise.

Strap

Cast on 37 sts.

Starting with a knit row work 3 rows in st st. Cast off in purl.

Making up

Seam the back of the hat. With right sides together, stitch the shaped edges of the peak. Turn right side out and sew the cast-off edge of the upper part of the peak to the lower edge of the hat, matching the centre fronts. Slip stitch the underside of the peak to the inside of the hat. Sew the strap in place, just above the peak, with the purl side up. Attach a button to each end of the strap.

This hat is full of love, accented with a silver streak. The simple design is appropriate for wearing any time – touring through the park on a skateboard or spending a night on the town.

Tattoo beanie

Size

One size fits most

Actual measurements

18in (46cm) circumference, 7in (18cm) height

Materials

Rowan Siena 4 ply 100% mercerized cotton (153yds/140m per 50g ball):

2 balls in 674 Black (A)

1 ball in 666 Chilli (B)

Rowan Shimmer 60% cupro, 40% polyester (191yds/175m per 25g ball):

1 ball in 093 Titanium (C)

A pair each of 2.75mm (UK12:US2) and 3mm (UK11:US-) needles

Darning needle

Tattoo beanie chart

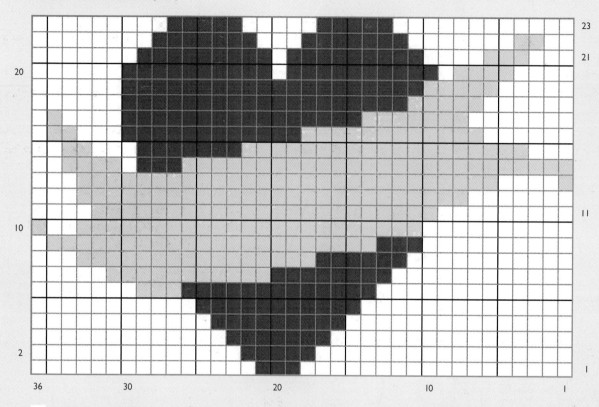

COLOUR A
COLOUR B
COLOUR C

Tension

28 sts and 38 rows to 4in (10cm) over st st using A and 3mm needles.
Use larger or smaller needles if necessary to obtain correct tension.

Method

This beanie begins with a 2 x 2 rib, and then continues in stocking stitch with an intarsia design worked in at the front.

Hat

Using 2.75mm needles and A, cast on 140 sts.
Work 1¼in (3cm) in k2, p2 rib, inc 1 st at end of last row (141 sts).

Change to 3mm needles.

Rows 1–8: Beg with a knit row, work 8 rows in st st.

Row 9 (RS): K52, knit row 1 of 36 st from right to left, k53.

Row 10: P53, purl row 2 of 36 sts of chart from left to right, p52.

Continue working from the chart following the odd rows in knit from right to left, and the even rows in purl from left to right until all 23 rows of the chart have been worked.

Next row: Starting with a purl row, continue in st st using A until work measures 5¾in (14.5cm) from cast-on edge.

Shape crown

Row 1 (dec): (K5, k2tog) to last st, k1 (121 sts).
Work 5 rows.

Row 7 (dec): (K4, k2tog) to last st, k1 (101 sts).
Work 5 rows.

Row 13 (dec): (K3, k2tog) to last st, k1 (81 sts).
Work 5 rows.

Row 19 (dec): (K2, k2tog) to last st, k1 (61 sts).
Work 1 row.

Break yarn and thread through remaining 61 sts. Draw up tightly and fasten off.

Making up

Join the back seam.

This wonderfully simple topper works up quickly in chunky yarn. It will cover your ears for warmth, and the oversized pompom makes a big statement!

Mega bobble

Size

One size fits most

Actual measurements

18⅞in (48cm) circumference, 8⅝in (22cm) height, excluding pompom

Materials

Rowan Big Wool, 100% merino wool (87yds/80m per 100g ball):

1 ball in 048 Linen

A pair of 10mm (UK000:US15) needles

Darning needle

Cardboard for making pompom

HATS

Tension

9 sts and 13 rows to 4in (10cm) over pattern using 10mm needles. Use larger or smaller needles if necessary to obtain correct tension.

Method

The hat is knitted back and forth in basket weave stitch with shaping at the crown, then seamed up the back. A large pompom using the rest of the yarn tops it off.

Hat

Cast on 40 sts.

Row 1 (WS): K4, (p2, k4) to end.
Row 2 (RS): P4 (k2, p4) to end.
Row 3: As row 1.
Row 4: As row 2.
Row 5 (WS): K2, (p2, k4) to last 2 sts, k2.
Row 6 (RS): P2, (k2, p4) to last 2 sts, p2.
Row 7: Rep row 5.
Row 8: Rep row 6.
These 8 rows form the pattern.
Rows 9–25: Rep 8-row pattern twice more, then work row 1 once more.

Shape crown

Row 26 (RS): *(P2tog) twice, k2tog. Rep from * to last 4 sts, (p2tog) twice (20 sts).
Row 27 (WS): (K2, p1) to last 2 sts, k2.
Row 28 (RS): (P2tog, k1) to last 2 sts, p2tog (13 sts).
Row 29 (WS): (K1, p1) to last st, k1.
Break yarn and thread through remaining 13 sts. Draw up tightly and fasten off.

Making up

Join the back seam carefully matching the basket weave pattern. Make a large pompom (see page 150) and attach to the top of the hat.

A triangle is transformed into a more interesting
and gentle shape with a couple of tucks and a fold.
Broken moss stitch adds lots of texture to this design.

Tucked cap

Size

One size fits most

Actual measurements

20in (51cm) circumference at bottom edge, 8¼in
(21cm) height

Materials

Jamieson & Smith Shetland Aran 100% Shetland wool
(98yds/90m per 50g ball):
2 balls in BSS71
A pair 4.5mm (UK7:US7) needles
Darning needle

Tension

15 sts and 20 rows to 4in (10cm) over pattern using 4.5mm needles. Use larger or smaller needles if necessary to obtain correct tension.

Method

The basic shape is knitted in pattern, then joined at the centre back and top. Two tucks finish the silhouette, and the tip of the hat is then folded over and stitched down.

Cap

Cast on 75 sts.

Rows 1 and 2: (K1, p1) to last st, k1.

Row 3: (K1, p1) to last st, k1.

Row 4: Purl.

Row 5: (P1, k1) to last st, p1.

Row 6: Purl.

Rep rows 3–6 three more times.

Shape top

Row 19: As row 3.

Row 20 (dec): P15, p2tog, p1, p2tog, p35, p2tog, p1, p2tog, p15 (71 sts).

Row 21: (P1, k1) 7 times, p2, k1, p2, (k1, p1) 16 times, k1, p2, k1, p2, (k1, p1) 7 times.

Row 22: Purl.

Row 23: (K1, p1) 7 times, k2, p1, k2, (p1, k1) 16 times, p1, k2, p1, k2, (p1, k1) 7 times.

Row 24 (dec): P14, p2tog, p1, p2tog, p33, p2tog, p1, p2tog, p14 (67 sts).

Row 25: As row 5.

Row 26: Purl.

Row 27: As row 3.

Row 28 (dec): P13, p2tog, p1, p2tog, p31, p2tog, p1, p2tog, p13 (63 sts).

Row 29: (P1, k1) 6 times, p2, k1, p2, (k1, p1) 14 times, k1, p2, k1, p2, (k1, p1), 6 times.

Row 30: Purl.

Row 31: (K1, p1) 6 times, k2, p1, k2, (p1, k1) 14 times, p1, k2, p1, k2, (p1, k1) 6 times.

Row 32 (dec): P12, p2tog, p1, p2tog, p29, p2tog, p1, p2tog, p12 (59 sts).

Row 33: As row 5.

Row 34: Purl.

Row 35: As row 3.

Row 36 (dec): P11, p2tog, p1, p2tog, p27, p2tog, p1, p2tog, p11 (55 sts).

Row 37: (P1, k1) 5 times, p2, k1, p2, (k1, p1) 12 times, k1, p2, k1, p2, (k1, p1) 5 times.

Row 38: Purl.

Row 39: (K1, p1) 5 times, k2, p1, k2, (p1, k1), 12 times, p1, k2, p1, k2, (p1, k1) 5 times.

Row 40 (dec): P10, p2tog, p1, p2tog, p25, p2tog, p1, p2tog, p10 (51 sts).

Row 41: As row 5.

Row 42: Purl.

Row 43: As row 3.

Row 44 (dec): P9, p2tog, p1, p2tog, p23, p2tog, p1, p2tog, p9 (47 sts).

Row 45: (P1, k1) 4 times, p2, k1, p2, (k1, p1) 10 times, k1, p2, k1, p2, (k1, p1), 4 times.

Row 46: Purl.

Row 47: (K1, p1) 4 times, k2, p1, k2, (p1, k1) 10 times, p1, k2, p1, k2, (p1, k1) 4 times.

Row 48 (dec): P8, p2tog, p1, p2tog, p21, p2tog, p1, p2tog, p8 (43 sts).

Row 49: As row 5.

Row 50: Purl.

Row 51: As row 3.

Row 52 (dec): P7, p2tog, p1, p2tog, p19, p2tog, p1, p2tog, p7 (39 sts).

Row 53: (P1, k1) 3 times, p2, k1, p2, (k1, p1) 8 times, k1, p2, k1, p2, (k1, p1) 3 times.

Row 54: Purl.

Row 55: (K1, p1) 3 times, k2, p1, k2, (p1, k1) 8 times, p1, k2, p1, k2, (p1, k1) 3 times.

Row 56 (dec): P6, p2tog, p1, p2tog, p17, p2tog, p1, p2tog, p6 (35 sts).

Row 57: As row 5.

Row 58: Purl.

Row 59: As row 3.

Row 60 (dec): P5, p2tog, p1, p2tog, p15, p2tog, p1, p2tog, p5 (31 sts).

Row 61: (P1, k1) twice, p2, k1, p2, (k1, p1) 6 times, k1, p2, k1, p2, (k1, p1) twice.

Row 62 (dec): P4, p2tog, p1, p2tog, p13, p2tog, p1, p2tog, p4 (27 sts).

Row 63: As row 3.

Row 64 (dec): P3, p2tog, p1, p2tog, p11, p2tog, p1, p2tog, p3 (23 sts).

Row 65: P1, k1, p2, k1, p2, (k1, p1) 4 times, k1, p2, k1, p2, k1, p1.

Row 66 (dec): P2, p2tog, p1, p2tog, p9, p2tog, p1, p2tog, p2 (19 sts).

Row 67: As row 3.

Row 68 (dec): (P1, p2tog) twice, p7, (p2tog, p1) twice (15 sts).

Row 69: P2, k1, p2, (k1, p1) twice, k1, p2, k1, p2.

Row 70 (dec): P2 tog, p1, p2tog, p5, p2tog, p1, p2tog (11 sts).

Cast off in k1, p1 pattern.

Making up

Seam the back and the cast-off edges at the top.

Make a horizontal tuck across the centre front, 4¾in (12cm) from the lower edge on the right side of the work, ½in (1.25cm) deep and 4in (10cm) long. Sew in place.

Make a second tuck in the same way 1½in (4cm) above the first. Sew in place.

Fold the top of the hat over so the tip of it sits inside the second tuck at the front. Sew in place.

Cleverly constructed flowers and picots decorate a band
of cables and bobbles. The band is knitted as a strip,
then stitches are picked up along the side for the crown.

Flapper

Size

One size fits most

Actual measurements

19¾in (50cm) circumference

Materials

Sublime Cashmere Merino Silk Aran 75% extra fine merino,
20% silk, 5% cashmere (94 yds/86m per 50g ball):
2 balls in 0017 Vintage Red (A)
1 ball in 0135 Bay (B)
A pair of 5mm (UK6:US8) needles
Cable needle
Approximately 15 beads/pearls
Sewing needle
Thread

Tension

21 sts and 24 rows to 4in (10cm) over pattern band using 5mm needles. Use larger or smaller needles if necessary to obtain correct tension.

Method

The cabled band is knitted in a strip and stitches are picked up along one side for the crown. Flowers and a picot braid are sewn to hat and embellished with beads.

Special abbreviations

t3b: Slip next st onto cable needle and hold at back of work, knit next 2 sts from left-hand needle, then purl 1 from cable needle.

t3f: Slip next 2 sts onto cable needle and hold at front of work, purl 1 from left-hand needle, then knit 2 from cable needle.

c5f: Slip next 3 sts onto cable needle and hold at front of work, knit next 2 sts from left-hand needle, slip the purl st from cable needle back onto left-hand needle, purl 1, then knit 2 from cable needle.

Pattern band
(this will be turned sideways when completed)

Using A cast on 19 sts. Working the background in reverse st st cont as follows.

Row 1 (WS): K4, *k into front, back, front, back and front of next st (bobble made)**, k2, p2, k1, p2, k2, rep from * to **, k4.

Row 2: P4, k5tog tbl (completing bobble), p2, c5f, p2, k5tog tbl, p4.

Row 3: K7, p2, k1, p2, k7.

Row 4: P6, t3b, p1, t3f, p6.

Row 5: K6, p2, k3, p2, k6.

Row 6: P5, t3b, p3, t3f, p5.

Row 7: K5, p2, k2, make bobble in next st (as on 1st row), k2, p2, k5.

Row 8: P4, t3b, p2, k5 tog tbl, p2, t3f, p4.

Row 9: K4, p2, k7, p2, k4.

Row 10: P3, t3b, p7, t3f, p3.

Row 11: K3, p2, k2, make bobble in next st, k3, make bobble in next st, k2, p2, k3.

Row 12: P2, t3b, p2, k5tog tbl, p3, k5tog tbl, p2, t3f, p2.

Row 13: K2, p2, k11, p2, k2.

Row 14: P2, k2, p11, k2, p2.

Row 15: K2, p2, k3, make bobble in next st, k3, make bobble in next st, k3, p2, k2.

Row 16: P2, t3f, p2, k5tog tbl, p3, k5tog tbl, p2, t3b, p2.

Row 17: K3, p2, k9, p2, k3.

Row 18: P3, t3f, p7, t3b, p3.

Row 19: K4, p2, k3, make bobble in next st, k3, p2, k4.

Row 20: P4, t3f, p2, k5tog tbl, p2, t3b, p4.

Row 21: K5, p2, k5, p2, k5.

Row 22: P5, t3f, p3, t3b, p5.

Row 23: K6, p2, k3, p2, k6.

Row 24: P6, t3f, p1, t3b, p6.

Repeat these 24 rows 4 times more.

Cast off.

Crown

With RS of work facing and using A, pick up and knit 75 sts along one long edge of the band.

Work in moss stitch pattern for 9 rows, dec 2 sts evenly spaced on last row (73 sts).

Continue in st st as follows.

Row 1 (RS): *K7, k2tog, rep from * to last st, k1 (65 sts).

Row 2 and every foll alt row: Purl.

Row 3: *K6, k2tog, rep from * to last st, k1 (57 sts).

Row 5: *K5, k2tog, rep from * to last st, k1 (49 sts).

Continue decreasing in this way, working 1 fewer st between the decs, until 17 sts remain, ending with a RS row.

Next row: P1, (p2tog) 8 times (9 sts).

Break yarn and thread through remaining sts. Do not fasten off.

Base of hat

With RS facing and using A, pick up and knit 75 sts along bottom edge and proceed in k1, p1 rib for 1in (2.5cm) ending with a WS row.

Using B work in k1, p1 rib for 2 rows. With right side facing work picot edge as follows:

*K2tog, yo, rep from * to last st, k1. Work 2 more rows in rib, cast off loosely. Turn under the last 2 rows and slip stitch on the underside, creating the picot effect on the edge.

Flower decoration
Large flower

Using B cast on 4 sts.

Row 1: K into front and back of each st (8 sts).

Rows 2, 4 and 6: Purl.

Row 3: Rep row 1 (16 sts).

Row 5: Rep row 1 (32 sts).

Row 7: Cast off 1 st, *sl1 st from right-hand needle to left-hand needle. Cast on 3 sts using the simple cast-on method, cast off 5 sts; rep from * until 1 st remains. Fasten off.

Gather cast-on edge in centre and fasten. Sew seam.

Small flower

Using A cast on 5 sts.

Row 1: K into front and back of each st (10 sts).

Rows 2 and 4: Purl.

Row 3: Rep row 1 (20 sts).

Row 5: Rep row 7 as for large flower. Complete as for large flower.

Stitch the small flower onto the large one and decorate with pearls/beads.

Picot braid

Using B *cast on 4 sts, cast off 3 sts, place remaining st back onto left-hand needle; rep from * 24 times or the length required. Cast on 1 st (25 sts). Cast off 1 st leaving 1 st on right-hand needle; **pick up strand lying between needles and k into the back of it; place st back on left-hand needle and pass 2nd st over 1st stitch; k1 and pass 1st st over 2nd st; rep from ** to end, fasten off.

Making up

Draw the yarn at top of the crown up tightly and carefully sew the back seam, matching patterns. Arrange picot braid and flowers together on the side of the hat and stitch in place.

You'll keep doubly warm in this colourful hat that also has a striped lining. The hat and lining are knitted separately, then joined along the lower edge of ribbing.

Cossack

Size
One size fits most
Actual measurements
22in (56cm) circumference

Materials
Rowan Felted Tweed DK 50% merino wool/25% alpaca/25% viscose (191yds/175m per 50g ball):
1 ball in 161 Avocado (A)
1 ball in 154 Ginger (B)
1 ball in 151 Bilberry (C)
1 ball in 150 Rage (D)
A pair each of 2.75mm (UK12:US2) and 3.25mm (UK10:US3) needles

Cossack chart

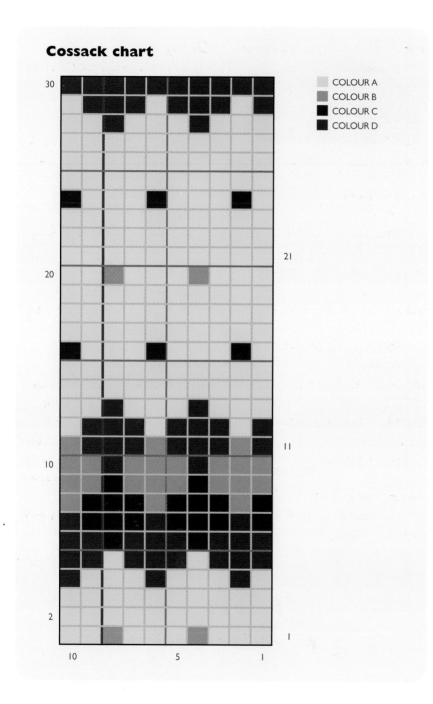

COLOUR A
COLOUR B
COLOUR C
COLOUR D

Tension

27 sts and 32 rows to 4in (10cm) over chart pattern using 3.25mm needles. Use larger or smaller needles if necessary to obtain correct tension.

Method

The colour pattern can be worked from the chart or the written instructions. A striped lining is knitted separately and slip stitched to the hat.

Hat

Using 2.75mm needles and B cast on 162 sts.

Row 1 (RS): With C, knit.

Row 2 (WS): *P1, k1, rep from * to end of row.

Work 5 more rows in k1, p1 rib ending with a RS row.

Change to 3.25mm needles. With A, beg with a purl row work 3 rows in st st.

Commence pattern

Continuing in st st and starting with row 1, follow the chart or written instructions below to work the 30-row pattern.

Row 1 (RS): (3A, 1B) to last 2 sts, 2A.

Rows 2 and 3: A.

Row 4: 1D, (3A, 1D) to last st, 1A.

Row 5: (3D, 1A) to last 2 sts 2D.

Row 6: 2D, (1C, 3D) to end.

Row 7: 1C, (1D, 3C) to last st 1D.

Row 8: (1B, 3C) to last 2 sts, 1B, 1C.

Row 9: (3B, 1C) to last 2 sts, 2B.

Row 10: 2B, (1D, 3B) to end.

Row 11: 1D, (1B, 3D) to last st, 1B.

Row 12: (1A, 3D) to last 2 sts, 1A, 1D.

Row 13: (3A, 1D) to last 2 sts, 2A.

Rows 14 and 15: A.

Row 16: (1C, 3A) to last 2 sts, 1C, 1A.

Rows 17–19: A.

Row 20: 2A, (1B, 3A) to end.

Rows 21–23: A.

Row 24: (1C, 3A) to last 2 sts, 1C, 1A.

Rows 25–27: A.

Row 28: 2A, (1D, 3A) to end.

Row 29: 1D, 1A, (3D, 1A) to end.

Row 30: D.

Using C work the next 3 rows in garter st. This forms the start of the crown.

Row 34 (WS): Purl with A.

Shape crown

Row 35: K1, (sl 1, k1, psso, k14) to last st, k1 (152 sts).

Row 36 and all alternate rows: Purl.

Row 37: K1, (sl 1, k1, psso, k13) to last st, k1 (142 sts).

Row 39: K1, (sl 1, k1, psso, k12) to last st, k1 (132 sts).

Row 41: K1, (sl 1, k1, psso, k11) to last st, k1 (122 sts).

Row 43: K1, (sl 1, k1, psso, k10) to last st, k1 (112 sts).

Row 45: K1, (sl 1, k1, psso, k9) to last st, k1 (102 sts).

Row 47: K1, (sl 1, k1, psso, k8) to last st, k1 (92 sts).

Row 49: K1, (sl 1, k1, psso, k7) to last st, k1 (82 sts).

Row 51: K1, (sl 1, k1, psso, k6) to last st, k1 (72 sts).

Row 53: K1, (sl 1, k1, psso, k5) to last st, k1 (62 sts).

Row 55: K1, (sl 1, k1, psso, k4) to last st, k1 (52 sts).

Row 57: K1, (sl 1, k1, psso, k3) to last st, k1 (42 sts).

Row 59: K1, (sl 1, k1, psso, k2) to last st, k1 (32 sts).

Row 61: K1, (sl 1, k1, psso, k1) to last st, k1 (22 sts).

Row 63: K1, (sl 1, k1, psso) to last st, k1 (12 sts).

Row 64: (P2 tog) to end of row (6 sts).

Break yarn and thread through remaining 6 sts. Draw up tightly and fasten off.

Lining

Using 2.75mm needles and C cast on 162 sts.

Knit 1 RS row.

Commence stripe pattern

Beg with a P row, cont in st st changing colours as follows:

Rows 1 and 2: B.

Rows 3 and 4: D.

Rows 5 and 6: C

Rep the 6-row stripe pattern 6 times, then work row 1 once more.

Shape crown

Maintaining the stripe pattern as set, follow the instructions for shaping the crown for the hat.

Making up

Sew in all the ends and then sew up the seams of the hat and the lining using back stitch or mattress stitch. Place the lining inside the hat with the lining seam at the opposite side to the seam of the hat, so that you don't have both seams on top of each other. Slip stitch the lining to the hat on the inside, at the edge of the rib.

Techniques

Getting started

Size

Because of the nature of knitted and crocheted hats and caps, those presented here are intended to fit most adults. A finished measurement is given with each project, and you can alter that measurement by using a thicker or thinner yarn.

Tension

Variations in tension can have a noticeable effect on the size of a finished hat. You can use a variation in tension to adjust the finished size, but if you want the given size, be sure you get the correct tension.

Materials and equipment

Needles and hooks

Most of the designs in this book are worked back and forth on standard knitting needles, a few are knitted in the round, and others are crocheted. Bamboo needles are useful if you are using a rough-textured yarn as they are very smooth and will help to prevent snags. You may also need double-pointed or circular needles. Where crochet hooks are used, these are standard metal hooks that are widely available.

Yarn

Hats may be made in a huge variety of yarns. Wool or wool-mix yarns have the best insulating properties. If you are using acrylic yarn, you may prefer to choose one of the bulkier designs.

Substituting yarn

It is relatively simple to substitute different yarns for any of the projects in this book. One way to do this is to work out how many wraps per inch (wpi) the yarn produces (see table). It is important to check tension, so begin by working a tension swatch. Then wind the yarn closely, in a single layer, round a rule or similar object, and count how many 'wraps' it produces to an inch (2.5cm). For a successful result, choose a yarn that produces twice, or slightly more than twice, the number of wraps per inch as there are stitches per inch in the tension swatch.

Tension required	Number of wraps per inch produced by yarn
8 sts per inch (4-ply)	16–18 wraps per inch
6.5 sts per inch (Double knitting)	13–14 wraps per inch
5.5 sts per inch (Chunky)	11–12 wraps per inch

Knitting techniques

Simple cast-on

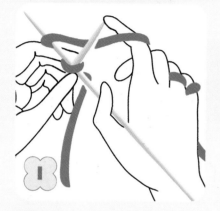

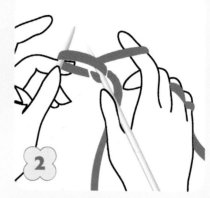

1 Form a slip knot by making a loop and pulling the free end of the yarn up through it to form a new loop. Put this on the left needle and pull the short end of the yarn to tighten. Insert the right needle into this loop and wrap yarn round it as shown.

2 Pull the yarn through the loop to create a new one.

3 Slide it on to the left-hand needle. There are now 2 sts on the left needle. Continue in this way until you have the required number of sts.

Cable cast-on

For a firmer edge, cast on the first 2 sts as shown above. When casting on the third and subsequent sts, insert the needle between the cast-on sts on the left needle, wrap the yarn round and pull through to create a loop. Slide the loop on to the left needle. Repeat to end.

Thumb method cast-on

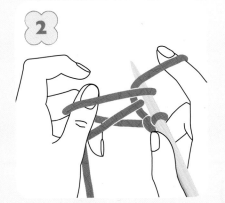

1 Make a slip knot some way from the end of the yarn and place on the needle. Pull the knot tight.

2 Hold needle in right hand and wrap the loose tail end round the left thumb, from front to back. Push the needle point through the thumb loop from front to back. Wind ball end of yarn round needle from left to right.

3 Pull the loop through thumb loop, then remove thumb. Gently pull the new loop tight using the tail yarn. Rep until the desired number of sts are on the needle.

Knit stitch

1 Hold the needle with the cast-on sts in your left hand. Place the tip of the empty right needle into the back of the first st and wrap the yarn round as for casting on.

2 Pull the yarn through to create a new loop.

3 Slip the newly made st on to the right needle. Continue in the same way for each st on the left-hand needle. To start a new row, turn the work to swap the needles and repeat steps.

Purl stitch

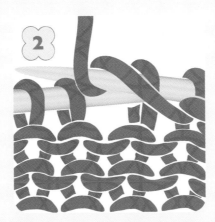

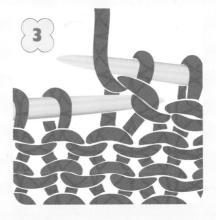

1 Hold the yarn at the front of the work as shown.

2 Place the right needle into the front of the first st. Wrap the yarn round the needle in an anti-clockwise direction as shown.

3 Bring the needle back through the st and pull through.

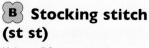

Other stitches

A **Garter stitch (g st)**

Knit every row.

B **Stocking stitch (st st)**

Knit on RS rows and purl on WS rows.

Reverse stocking stitch (rev st st): Purl on RS rows and knit on WS rows.

C **Moss stitch (m st)**

With an even number of sts:

Row 1: (K1, p1) to end.

Row 2: (P1, k1) to end.

Rep rows 1 and 2 for pattern.

With an odd number of sts:

Row 1: *K1, p1, rep from * to last st, k1.

Rep to form pattern.

D **Single (1 x 1) rib**

With an even number of sts:

Row 1: *K1, p1, rep from * to end.

Rep for each row.

With an odd number of sts:

Row 1: *K1, p1, rep from * to last st, k1.

Row 2: *P1, k1, rep from * to last st, p1.

E **Double (2 x 2) rib**

With a multiple of 4 sts:

Row 1: *K2, p2, rep from * to end.

Rep for each row.

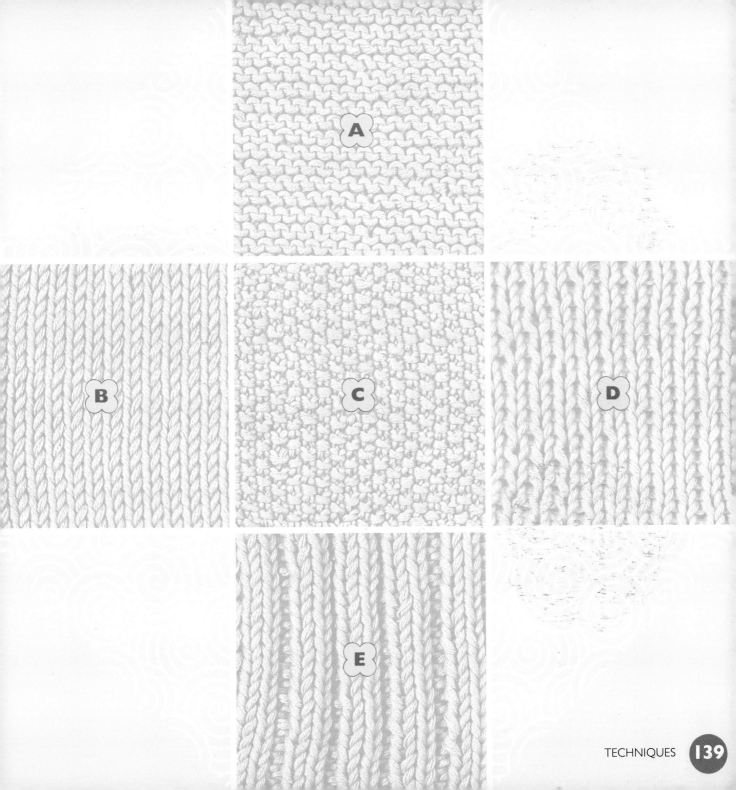

Colour knitting

Intarsia

Blocks of colour are created by using the intarsia technique of twisting the yarns together at the back of the work with each colour change (see diagram). It is better to use bobbins than whole balls to prevent tangling. They are smaller and can hang at the back of the work out of the way. Once finished, ends are woven in at the back, and pressing under a damp cloth will help to neaten any distorted stitches.

Reading charts

Most knitting charts are shown in squares, with each square representing one stitch. Charts are usually marked in sections of ten stitches, which makes counting easier.

When working in stocking stitch on straight needles, read the chart from right to left on knit (RS) rows and from left to right on purl (WS) rows. Check carefully after every purl row to make sure that the pattern stitches are in the correct position.

Fair Isle

Fair Isle knitting uses the stranding technique, which involves picking up and dropping yarns as they are needed. Unlike intarsia, they are then carried across the row. Loops are formed along the back of the work, but these should not exceed about 5 sts in length. Make sure the loops are of an even tension or the fabric may pucker.

1 Begin by knitting with the first colour (A), which is dropped when you need to incorporate the second (B). To pick up A again, bring it under B and knit again.

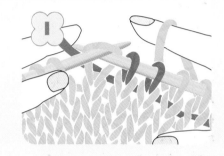

2 To pick up B again, drop A and bring B over A, then knit again.

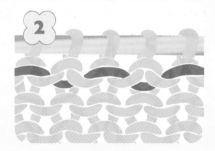

Pick up and knit

 With RS facing, insert the needle under both strands of the edge stitch. Wrap the yarn around the needle.

 Knit the picked-up stitch.

Working with double-pointed needles (dpns)

Using double-pointed needles is a way of working in the round and usually involves using four or five needles. One needle is always kept aside as the 'working needle'.

1 Divide the number of stitches to be cast on by the number of needles (not including the working needle). So if using a set of four dpns, divide the number of stitches by three. If you have only a small number of stitches to cast on, then it may be easier to do this on one needle and then slip them across afterwards. Put a stitch marker on the first stitch so that you can see where the round starts and ends.

2 Knit across the stitches from each needle, taking care not to twist the cast-on row and slipping the stitch marker across when it is reached. As you empty each needle it becomes your working needle for the next section. Continue working the stitches in this way as required.

Casting off

1 Knit 2 sts on to the right-hand needle, then slip the first st over the second st and let it drop off the needle so that 1 st remains.

2 Knit another st so you have 2 sts on the right-hand needle again. Rep process until there is only 1 st on the left needle. Break yarn and thread through rem st to fasten off. To cast off purlwise (p-wise), follow the same process, but with purl stitches.

Crochet techniques

Chain stitch (ch)

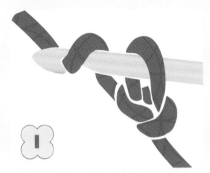

1

2

1 Form a slip knot on the hook by making a loop and pulling the free end of the yarn up through it to form a new loop. With hook in right hand and yarn resting over middle finger of left hand, pull yarn taut. Take hook under, then over yarn.

2 Pull the hook and yarn through the loop while holding slip knot steady. Rep to form a foundation row of chain stitch (ch).

Chain stitch is the usual base for other crochet stitches and is also useful for making simple ties.

Double crochet (dc)

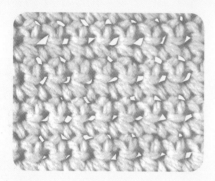

Double crochet produces a dense fabric that is ideal for lining, while single rows are ideal for edging.

1 Place hook into a st. Wrap yarn round hook and draw the loop back through the work towards you.

2 There should now be two loops on the hook. Wrap yarn round hook again, then draw through both loops, leaving one loop on the hook. One double crochet (dc) now complete. Rep to continue row.

Slip stitch (ss)

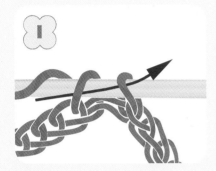

1 This stitch can be used to join a round. Slip the crochet hook under the top two strands of the V of the first stitch of the row.

2 Wrap the yarn around the hook and draw it back through both the V and the loop on the hook.

Half treble (h tr)

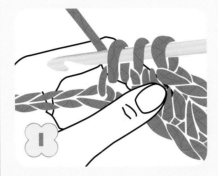

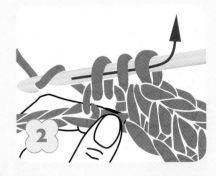

1 Wrap yarn around hook and then place into a stitch. Wrap yarn around hook and then draw the loop through. Three loops should now be on the hook.

2 Wrap yarn around hook again and draw through the three loops. There should be one loop remaining on the hook.

Treble crochet (tr)

Crochet worked in half-treble and treble stitch has a more open weave than double crochet.

1 Follow instructions for half treble until you have three loops on the hook. Catch the yarn and draw through two of the loops.

2 Catch yarn again and draw it through the remaining two loops.

Finishing touches

Sewing up

Mattress stitch

Place the pieces to be joined on a flat surface, laid together side by side with right sides towards you. Using matching yarn, thread a needle back and forth with small, straight stitches. The stitches form a ladder between the two pieces of fabric, creating a flat, secure seam.

Stocking stitch joins

The edges of stocking stitch tend to curl, so they may be tricky to join. The best way to join them is to use mattress stitch to pick up the bars between the columns of stitches.

Working upwards or downwards according to preference, secure the yarn to one of the pieces you want to join. Place the edges of the work together and pick up a bar from one side, then pick up the corresponding bar from the opposite side. Repeat. After a few stitches, pull gently on the yarn and the two sides will come together in a seam that is almost invisible. Take care to stay in the same column all the way. Do not pull the stitches tight at first as you will not be able to see what you are doing.

Garter stitch joins

It is easier to join garter stitch as it has a firm edge and lies flat. Place the edges of the work together, right side up, and see where the stitches line up. Pick up the bottom loops of the stitches on one side of the work and the top loops of the stitches on the other side. After a few stitches, pull gently on the yarn. The stitches should lock together and lie completely flat. The inside of the join should look the same as it does on the outside.

Slip stitch

Insert a threaded tapestry needle into a stitch on the wrong side of the knitting and then into the cast-on edge of the hem. Moving from right to left, work stitch by stitch and repeat for the length of the hem.

Pompoms

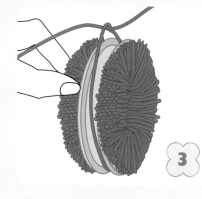

1 Cut out two cardboard circles a little smaller in diameter than the size of pompom you want to make. Make a hole in the middle of both, about a third of the diameter. Put both circles together and, using lengths of yarn, thread through the middle and begin wrapping around the outer edge until your card is completely covered. Use one or more colours for different effects. Continue working in this way until the centre hole is only a pinprick.

2 With sharp-ended scissors, cut all around the edge of the circle, slicing through all the strands of yarn.

3 Now ease a length of yarn between the card discs and tie very firmly around the centre, leaving a tail for sewing. You have now secured all the strands of yarn around the middle. Ease the card discs away from the pompom and fluff out all the strands. Trim off any loose or straggly ends.

Fringing

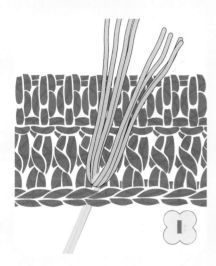

1 Cut a piece of stiff card so the height is the required length of your fringing. Wind your yarn around it – the number of times depends on how thick your fringe will be. Cut through the yarn at one edge of the card. Select the number of lengths of yarn you need for each tassel and fold them in half. Insert a crochet hook from the WS to the RS of the work where the fringe is to be positioned and hook the folded yarn.

2 Draw the yarn some of the way through the work.

3 Now draw the cut ends through the loop to tighten. Trim ends.

Tasses

1 Cut a piece of stiff card so the height is the required length of your tassel. Wrap the yarn round it several times, depending on how full you require the tassel to be. Secure this bundle with a separate length of yarn threaded through at one end, and tied leaving long ends. Cut through the bundle at the opposite edge.

2 Keeping the strands folded in half, remove the card. About a quarter of the way down from the fold, wind a separate length of yarn a few times round the whole bundle, including the long ends of the tie, to form the head of the tassel. Tie the two ends of this length of yarn together tightly. Trim all the ends of yarn at the base of the tassel to give a tidy finish.

Abbreviations

alt	alternate
approx	approximately
beg	begin, beginning
ch	chain stitch
cm	centimetre
cont	continue
dc	double crochet
dec	decrease(ing)
dpns	double-pointed needles
foll	following
g st	garter stitch, knit every row
htr	half treble crochet
in	inch(es)
inc	increase(ing)
K/k	knit
k-wise	knitwise, as if to knit
k2tog	knit two stitches together

k3tog	knit three stitches together
m	metre
m st	moss stitch
M1	make 1: pick up loop before next st and k it through back of loop
mm	millimetres
P/p	purl
p2tog	purl two stitches together
patt	pattern
psso	pass slipped stitch over
p-wise	purlwise, as if to purl
rem	remaining
rep	repeat
rev st st	reverse stocking stitch
RS	right side
sk	skip
sl	slip
sp(s)	space(s)
ss	slip stitch

ssk	slip 1 k-wise, slip 1 p-wise; knit these 2 stitches together through the back of the loops
st(s)	stitch(es)
st st	stocking stitch
tbl	through back of loop
tog	together
tr	treble crochet
wk	work
WS	wrong side
yb	yarn to back
yd	yard
yf	yarn to front
yo	yarn over needle
yrh	yarn round hook
*	work instructions following *, then repeat as directed
( )	repeat instructions inside brackets as directed

Conversions

Knitting needle sizes

UK	Metric	US
12	2.75mm	2
11	3mm	–
10	3.25mm	3
–	3.5mm	4
9	3.75mm	5
8	4mm	6
7	4.5mm	7
6	5mm	8

Crochet hook sizes

UK	Metric	US
12	2.5mm	C/2
11	3mm	–
10	3.25mm	D/3
9	3.5mm	E/4
8	4mm	G/6
7	4.5mm	7
6	5mm	H/8

UK/US crochet terms

UK	US
Double crochet	Single crochet
Half treble	Half double crochet
Treble	Double crochet
Double treble	Triple crochet
Treble treble	Double triple crochet

UK/US yarn weights

UK	US
2-ply	Lace
3-ply	Fingering
4-ply	Sport
Double knitting	Light worsted
Aran	Fisherman/worsted
Chunky	Bulky
Super chunky	Extra bulky

Acknowledgements

Photographer: Chris Gloag
Model: Alison King at MOT
Stylist: Jeni Dodson
Still-life photography: Anthony Bailey

Hat designs: Christine Boulton (page 122), Lisa Clayton (page 26), Janis Clinton (page 82), Charmaine Fletcher (pages 10 and 39), Debbie Gore (page 127), Stephanie

Offer (page 18) and Vanessa Mooncie
Charts and pattern checking: Sue Culligan and Jude Roust
Technique illustrations: Simon Rodway